Critical Reasoning
and Philosophy

Critical Reasoning and Philosophy

A Concise Guide to Reading, Evaluating, and Writing Philosophical Works

M. Andrew Holowchak

ROWMAN & LITTLEFIELD PUBLISHERS, INC.
Lanham • Boulder • New York • Toronto • Oxford

ROWMAN & LITTLEFIELD PUBLISHERS, INC.

Published in the United States of America
by Rowman & Littlefield Publishers, Inc.
A wholly owned subsidiary of The Rowman & Littlefield Publishing Group, Inc.
4501 Forbes Boulevard, Suite 200, Lanham, Maryland 20706
www.rowmanlittlefield.com

PO Box 317
Oxford
OX2 9RU, UK

British Library Cataloguing in Publication Information Available

Library of Congress Cataloging-in-Publication Data

Holowchak, Andrew, 1958-
  Critical reasoning & philosophy : a concise guide to reading,
evaluating, and writing philosophical works / M. Andrew Holowchak.
      p. cm.
Includes bibliographical references (p.   ) and index.
  ISBN 0-7425-3425-1 (hardcover) — ISBN 0-7425-3426-X (pbk.)
  1. Reasoning. I. Title: Critical reasoning and philosophy. II. Title.

  BC177.H653 2004
  107'.2 — dc22

                          2003021814

Printed in the United States of America

♾ ™ The paper used in this publication meets the minimum requirements of
American National Standard for Information Sciences — Permanence of Paper
for Printed Library Materials, ANSI/NISO Z39.48-1992

To Angela, for her support in all things and especially throughout this project, and to my many "mullet" friends at Muscle's.
Semper mulleti mulletant.

Contents

Preface

John Dewey said, "[I]t is no exaggeration to say that the measure of a civilization is the degree in which the method of cooperative intelligence replaces the method of brute conflict." This is a powerful and moving statement to the effect that people are civilized only inasmuch as they adopt both a critical and cooperative attitude toward solving problems.

The ancient Greek philosopher Socrates was perhaps the earliest to recognize this point. Never claiming to know anything, he spent most of his life in a cooperative search for truth, as he actively pursued knowledge with all who would search with him. In doing so, Socrates fashioned a dialectical method of cooperative inquiry that is, in some form or another, increasingly used in classrooms across the globe today.

In the nineteenth century, John Stuart Mill championed a similar method in his search for answers to religious, moral, philosophical, and political questions. Mill stated:

> Truth, in the great practical concerns of life, is so much a question of the reconciling and combining of opposites that very few have minds sufficiently capacious and impartial to make the adjustment with an approach to correctness, and it has to be made by the rough process of a struggle between combatants fighting under hostile banners.[1]

For any hope of success on unsettled issues, Mill believed that diversity of thought, the capacity for free expression of opinion, and an admission of fallibility by all involved were needed for progress. Any attempt to silence an opinion, he added, even one that was generally believed to be false, was an impediment to progress.

Prompted by the work of such pioneers, today researchers are coming increasingly to see the value of using critical and cooperative models of learning in classrooms. Such models are of special importance in classes on philosophy, which, much more than most other classes, challenge students to develop a critical attitude toward everyday-life issues.

Critical Reasoning and Philosophy: A Concise Guide to Reading, Evaluating, and Writing Philosophical Works is the culmination of several years of thinking about an integrative, cooperative, and critical approach to teaching introductory courses in philosophy. Philosophers are wedded to a specific type of analytic methodology that requires the honing and use of critical-reasoning skills at different levels: on the one hand, recognizing, reconstructing, and evaluating arguments (usually, those of other philosophers); on the other hand, being able to express themselves philosophically in coherent and tightly argued essays that move philosophical debate forward, however slowly. Students being introduced to philosophy need exposure to these skills and cannot fully appreciate the need for philosophical analysis without them.

Thus, I have created this text to complement most introductory-level philosophy courses. Its aims, as the title suggests, are to teach students how to read, evaluate, and write philosophy. The book begins analytically by giving students the tools and skills to recognize, break down, and analyze arguments before formally responding to them in writing. It ends synthetically in that, by a book's end, students will have learned how to advance and defend a philosophical position of their own in a critical essay.

The text comprises six sections, each of which contains a number of modules (nineteen in all). These modules are short, self-teaching units that are designed to make critical evaluation of philosophy user-friendly. The large number of modules and small size of each make, I hope, for ready and easy assimilation of the material. Section One looks at introductory issues through three modules (one on philosophy, one on critical reasoning, and one on how to read philosophy). Section Two concerns recognition and reconstruction of arguments in two modules. Section Three comprises two modules on diagramming arguments. The fourth section, on argument evaluation, has five modules that concern principles and components of evaluation, common deductive and inductive arguments, and common fallacies. Section Five, which is mostly non-philosophical in scope, looks at tips for proper writing in four modules. There are three modules in the final section: one on evaluative essays (focusing on evaluating a philosophical view), one on critical essays (focusing on defending a thesis of one's own), and one on a much neglected topic in philosophy classes—revising and rewriting essays.

The nineteen modules are complemented by five appendices. Appendix A offers some practice exercises for argument diagramming from famous philosophers. Appendices B and C give, respectively, a sample evaluative essay and a sample critical essay in an attempt to illustrate the principles and suggestions in the final section. These samples are taken from actual essays from students. Appendices D and E complement the final module on revising and rewriting essays. Appendix D is a sample comment sheet that offers guidelines for students to critically analyze each other's papers. Appendix E is a plan-for-revision sheet that offers guidelines for revising an essay that protects students from beginning a hasty revision.

Overall, I have used drafts of these modules in my introductory courses and have found them to be very helpful tools. I am confident that, even if students *cannot* distinguish Aristotle from aerosol years after one of my introductory courses, they'll remember many things about what makes an argument good (or bad) and they'll be capable of using these in their everyday-life decisions. I am sure that other philosophers, especially those who find content-based-only approaches to introductory courses on philosophy too limited, will discover that *Critical Reasoning and Philosophy* is a valuable and effective complement to their courses.

There are a number of other books on the market with similar aims. Many of these are fine books (I list some in my bibliography), yet I have found none that balances concern for reading, evaluating, and writing philosophy in a compendious, user-friendly format—hence, the motivation for writing my own book. In addition, I have chosen a module-based approach to this book so as to introduce students to critical-reasoning skills in *short, digestible units* that can be learned piecemeal and spread out over the course of a term.

HOW TO USE *CRITICAL REASONING AND PHILOSOPHY*

Below I give a sample syllabus from an actual class on Introduction to Philosophy, which was based on the themes education and pedagogical reform.

Introduction to Philosophy

I) Course Description: I have structured this course with a dual purpose: to introduce you to the vital discipline of philosophy and to develop and hone critical reasoning skills. To best bring these dual aims about, only two issues, education and pedagogical reform, will be our objects of philosophical investigation. Through the writings of many different philosophers, we'll critically examine questions such as *What is learning?*, *What ought to be the aims of education?*, and *How can we best facilitate the aims of education?*

Throughout the course, you will learn critical-reasoning skills in a stepwise fashion. We begin analytically. The first quarter of the course will focus on developing skills in argument recognition, reconstruction, and evaluation. We end synthetically. Drawing from the various works we examine through the term, you are required to develop your own thoughts on education and pedagogical reform and how these relate to human betterment in a four-page paper.

II) Course Objectives: Overall, I have designed this course principally to help you develop independent thought based on critical analysis of the material. An important step in this process is clear recognition of the merits as well as the limits and defects of your own position on a philosophic issue. Learning to respect well-thought-out positions contrary to your own is, therefore, essential to your own philosophical development. Of course, nothing rules out having fun along the way.

One crucially important point: In our critical analysis of material, we shall be earnestly seeking, to the best of our abilities, answers to these intriguing philosophical questions.

III) Daily Preparation of Class: In this course, we shall read and critically discuss several authors, each of whom gives us intriguing answers to the questions we pose above. You are expected to have done the weekly readings (listed below) before each lecture/discussion so that you may be able to critically discuss each thinker's views during our weekly sessions. Do not skim or speed-read. Read all prefaces, commentaries, and footnotes. Always bring the relevant text to class each day.

IV) Class Participation/Discussions: Come to class prepared to ask questions and discuss the weekly readings. Your views on the material need not conform to mine or to those of anyone else. Feel free to openly disagree with me or with other classmates, but do so *respectfully*! Since one of the goals of this course is to help you develop independent thought based on critical analysis of the material, as instructor, I'll often challenge you to develop a line of thought. In doing so, the view that I take may not be my own. Overall, quality of your comments is more important than quantity. Think things through!

Week One: A) Recognizing & Formatting Arguments
Sept.   4:   Introduction *(Modules 1 & 2)*
        5:    Greek History *(Module 3)*
        6:    Plato and Socrates: Begin *Laches*

Week Two: A) Recognizing Arguments
       10:    Plato: *Laches (Module 4)*
       11:    Plato: *Laches*
       12:    Plato: *Laches (Module 5)*
       13:    Presentation 1: *Socratic Dialectic in* Laches (Analytic Assignment 1)

Week Three: A) Reconstructing Arguments
       17:    Plato: *Charmides (Module 6)* (AA1 due)
       18:    Plato: *Charmides*
       19:    Plato: *Charmides (Module 7)*
       20:    Presentation 2: *Socratic Dialectic in* Charmides (Analytic Assignment 2)

Week Four: B) Analyzing Arguments
       24:    Sextus: Introduction *(Module 8)* (AA2 due)
       25:    Sextus: Book I
       26:    Sextus: Book I *(Module 9)*
       27:    Sextus: Book I (Analytic Assignment 3)

Week Five: B) Analyzing Arguments
Oct.   1:   Presentation 3: *Skepticism and Education* (AA3 due)
        2:    Mill: Introduction *(Module 10)*
        3:    Mill: Chapter I
        4:    Mill: Chapter II *(Modules 11 & 12)* (Analytic Assignment 4)

Week Six: B) Analyzing Arguments
    8:   Mill: Chapter II (AA4 due)
    9:   Mill: Chapter III *(Modules 13 & 14)*
  10:   Mill: Chapter III
  11:   Mill: Chapter IV (Evaluative Essay 1)

Week Seven: C) Evaluating Arguments
  15:   Mill: Chapter IV (EE1 due)
  16:   Mill: Chapter V *(Module 17)*
  17:   Presentation 4: *Millean Dialectic and Education*
  18:   *(Module 16)* (Evaluative Essay 2)

Week Eight: C) Evaluating Arguments
  22:   Dewey: Chapter I & II (EE2 due) *(Module 15)*
  23:   Dewey: Chapters III
  24:   Dewey: Chapters IV & V *(Module 18)*
  25:   Dewey: Chapters VI-VIII (Evaluative Essay 3)

Week Nine: C) Evaluating Arguments
  29:   Presentation 5: *Dewey on Educational Reform* (EE3 due)
        (Module 16)
  30:   Luke & Gore: Reading 3
  31:   Luke & Gore: Reading 3 *(Module 19)*
Nov.   1:   Luke & Gore: Reading 3 (Evaluative Essay 4)

Week Ten: D) Synthesis
  5:   Presentation 6: *Luke on Radical Pedagogy* (EE4 due)
  6:   Luke & Gore: Reading 8
  7:   Luke & Gore: Reading 8
  8:   Presentation 7: *Kenway & Modra on Feminist Pedagogy*

Week Eleven:
  12:   Holiday
  13:   Class Discussion (Journals and Synthetic Essays Due)

V) Texts:
1. Plato: *Laches and Charmides*
2. Sextus Empiricus: *Selections*

3. John Stuart Mill: *On Liberty*
4. John Dewey: *Experience and Education*
5. Luke and Gore: *Feminisms and Critical Pedagogy*
6. Holowchak: *Critical Reasoning and Philosophy*

Always bring the appropriate book to class for each meeting.

VI) Grading and Attendance: Your grade will be determined by (1) your reconstruction of arguments in the four analytic assignments (20%), your outline and essay in each of the four evaluative essays (20%), your final synthetic essay and outline (20%), (4) your participation in a discussion panels (20%), and your reaction journal (20%). Classes will be geared to guide you through the readings and prepare you for the workshops, essays, and discussion panels. *Thus, material will be given in class that is not covered in the required text.* So, though attendance is not mandatory, missing classes will certainly have an adverse affect on your grade.

For the discussion-panel grade, your peers will determine half of your grade. Each *non*-participating classmate will submit a group grade (and comments) for the panel as a whole and the mean of these grades will be one-half of the grade for each of the individuals on the panel. The other one-half will be given individually by me. The mean of these two scores will be your discussion-panel grade. Here you will be graded on content (50%) as well as creativity (25%) and on your visible commitment toward working together in a group-related project (25%). Your classmates comments will be made available to you. (In some cases, you will receive extra credit for insightful comments concerning discussion panels.)

VI.A) Analytic Workshops/Analytic Assignments: Analytic workshops are designed to develop and hone skills in argument recognition and reconstruction. For each workshop, you will have read all of the required material and come to class with a reconstruction of a particular argument in Standard Form (which we shall learn in class). In the main, these arguments will be relatively lengthy and implicit premises may be needed to make the link between premises and conclusion obvious. Each of the four standard-form reconstructions is worth 5% (20%) of your final grade.

VI.B) <u>Evaluative Papers</u>: There are four evaluative essays due (one page each) for each of the four evaluative workshops. Each of these papers will require an outline (on a separate page). Here I expect that, in addition to analytic skills involved in argument reconstruction, you will be developing evaluative skills. Consequently, at least half of your paper will be a critical analysis of the argument you flesh out. Together these essays account for 20% of your final grade.

VI.C) <u>Synthetic Essay</u>: For your synthetic essay, you are expected to draw critically from all of the readings and then *develop your own views* on learning and pedagogy in a coherent essay. Try not to do too much, but I expect you to have something novel to say here. Overall, this essay accounts for 20% of your final grade.

Grading for evaluative and synthetic papers will be as follows:
    15% for a clearly articulated thesis;
    15% for use of text;
    15% for structure and coherence;
    15% for grammar, spelling, and related problems; and
    40% for cogency of arguments on behalf of your thesis.

VI.D) <u>Discussion Panels</u>: For each group, you *must* meet with me and discuss the format for what you propose to do *at least* two weeks prior to your presentation. Therefore, advanced preparation is crucial here. As a group, your goal is to elaborate *relevantly* on the appropriate reading(s) in a manner that *goes beyond* what was presented in lecture and discussed in class. Try, as a group, to reach a consensus of opinion. Creativity is very important, but stay within the parameters of what we are trying to accomplish. While presenting, try to *actively* engage your peers in the classroom. You will be graded here for creativity (25%), demonstrated ability to work together (25%), and content (50%). I'll assign discussion panels on the very first day of class. Those who do not attend this session will be assigned a panel by or in consultation with me at a later time. Your discussion panel accounts for 20% of your grade.

VI.E) <u>Reaction Journals</u>: I require that you keep a journal in which you jot down your thoughts on the assigned readings as you do the readings.

You may write as little or as much as you want, and there are no guidelines concerning just what you write other than the requirement that each entry be philosophically relevant. Stream-of-consciousness style is fine. Date and label each entry (e.g., Plato's *Laches,* 2-6-01) prior to writing. Overall, your journal will account for the final 20% of your grade, so be sure that you make your entries in a timely fashion and that you put sufficient effort into them. *Bring your journals to class each day.* I'll collect these *randomly.* (If I collect your journals on a given day and you do not have an entry for the assigned reading of that day, you will receive no points for that entry. This is equivalent to missing an assignment!) Journals are required as a means of seeing to it that you do the readings for class *ahead of time.* They also afford you a preliminary means of ordering your thoughts on a particular reading before coming to class for discussion. My preference is that you use a small, spiral-bound notebook and a pen. Please write legibly!

NOTE

1. Mill 1978, 110.

Section One

INTRODUCTORY ISSUES

Module One

What Is Philosophy?

1) DEFINING PHILOSOPHY

Traditionally and I might even say superficially, "philosophy" has been defined as the "love of wisdom," and "philosophers" as "lovers of wisdom." This at least is what we find when we look into the etymology of the words. (The Greek word *philein* means "to like" or "to love" and *sophia* means "wisdom.") These definitions, however, do not help much in telling us just what it is that philosophers do. Many people, I suppose, believe that philosophers are rather disagreeable people, who saunter about and try to show others that they have no grounds for anything they happen to hold true. Others maintain, as I have often heard, that everyone is a philosopher to some degree.

While it is certainly true that philosophers argue much of the time and that all people discuss philosophical issues some of the time, it is not true that philosophers argue ceaselessly to no fruitful end or that everyone is a philosopher. There is a point to philosophical "contentiousness": Philosophical argument attempts to clarify matters by ridding of ambiguity and vagueness in everyday language. What's the payoff? A better understanding of the issues and perhaps even a solution to some stubborn problem.

All of us recognize the vital importance of the various arts and sciences. Art and its various means of expression add fullness, variety, beauty, and even flavor to our lives. Science continually makes discoveries that contribute to our health and our comfort. We take art and science for granted, yet the thought of what life would be like without either of these is too gruesome for most of us to entertain.

3

However, have you ever stopped to consider what makes art so special to us or why we trust the discoveries of the sciences? If you have, then you have taken at least a rudimentary interest in philosophy. Philosophy takes what seems plainly true or obvious and subjects it to scrutiny for the sake of deeper understanding. For instance, we take it for granted when a study suggests that vitamin E slows aging and guards against cancer. What, after all, do we really know about science? Because of ignorance or a sense of security in thinking that others may have the answers that we do not have, often we blindly follow when authorities like scientists speak.

However, the study of philosophy gives us the analytic tools to dissect what scientists do and open it to critical examination. Moreover, what it does to science, it does to all other disciplines. Philosophy takes our most fundamental principles and beliefs and asks us for a justification of them. It invites us to ask questions such as: What, if anything, is the best form of political life for humans? How ought we to live our lives? Does God exist? Behind the veneer of things that continually change, is anything eternally unchanging? What is love? What is beauty? Philosophy, then, is the science of sciences.

2) METHODS OF PHILOSOPHY

Why do we engage in philosophy? Perhaps no better answer exists than that given by Aristotle in the fourth century b.c.: We are naturally curious animals. Yet to engage in philosophy is not merely a matter of being curious about things. It requires that our curiosity be expressed through questions and answers in a manner that is both systematic and critical. To this end, however, the methods of philosophy are many. I enumerate some of the most important below.

Philosophy is analytic in that it analyzes the most basic assumptions that we use in an attempt to understand ourselves and the world around us.
Philosophy is normative in that it appeals to rules or precepts that determine correct and incorrect ways of human thinking and behavior.
Philosophy is critical in that it challenges time-honored cannons of belief in an effort to get at truth or further our understanding of some issue.

Philosophy is synthetic in that it aims to synthesize our views of ourselves and the world in a coherent and systematic manner.

Philosophy is rational in that it insists that reasons be given for what we believe and that consistency, simplicity, coherence, and order of thoughts are desirable.

Philosophy is creative in that it invites us to explore and examine new ways of looking at philosophical problems and issues.

3) TRADITIONAL BRANCHES OF PHILOSOPHY

Philosophy has historically been divided into five chief sub-disciplines: metaphysics, epistemology, aesthetics, ethics, and logic.

The study of what is real is called metaphysics. Metaphysics is an attempt at a coherent account of all that exists; the study of the most general and pervasive characteristics of the universe; or the study of ultimate reality.

The study of knowledge is called epistemology. Epistemology examines the origins, presuppositions, nature, extent, and validity of knowledge.

The study of beauty and related concepts is called aesthetics. Aesthetics asks questions such as: What is art? Are all beautiful things equally beautiful? Is there such a thing as aesthetic sensibility?

The study of morality or the best manner of living is called ethics. Ethics examines concepts related to practical reasoning, such as freedom of will, choice, virtue, duty, good, and right.

The study of the principles of reasoning is called logic. Logic is a normative discipline that is used as a tool for all sciences, even philosophy.

Yet today philosophers study a diverse field of practical issues from feminism and race relations to conflict resolution and death. In a sense, philosophers take many of the same questions that arise with respect to the "big five" and apply these to a broad array of today's topics of study.

Module Two

Philosophy and Critical Reasoning

1) APPLIED PHILOSOPHY

Applied philosophy is a non-traditional approach to philosophical in-quiry in that its subject matter draws from everyday-life concerns. Con-temporary issues in applied philosophy are in the areas of sex and love, politics, gender, race, environmental matters, medical ethics, peace and conflict resolution, and sport, to name just some.

Why is there a need for applied philosophy? The reason is simple. We benefit greatly by applying philosophical methods to the issues that confront us in our daily lives. Today, there is a wealth of information at our disposal on issues like drug-use among teens, AIDS, globaliza-tion, and gender equality. Unsurprisingly, these issues also invite rig-orous debate, even among experts, which makes it seem unreasonable, even irresponsible, to speak with absolute certainty on them. Take the morality of cloning. Many of us feel an undeniable repugnance for this technology. Our repugnance seems grounded by certain "intuitively correct" feelings that cloning is morally wrong. Yet it is difficult to put into words just why this is so. Repugnance, of course, is no justifica-tion for moral incorrectness. Still, we must make decisions on such is-sues or leave them in the hands of others to decide them for us. And it seems clear that a society is better off when it allows all its adult mem-bers to deliberate on such issues, since such issues impact all members of the society. To participate fully and most responsibly in them one needs a critical attitude.

2) WHAT IS A CRITICAL ATTITUDE?

Everyone has a unique depiction of the way the world is. For some, this picture is fixed through an uncritical acceptance of some notion of how things are that is perhaps handed down to them through religion or their parents. Such unreflective people are seldom concerned with the correctness of their picture; instead they are generally content just to have a picture, whether it is coherent or incoherent. Unreflective acceptance would be fine, of course, if there weren't so many religions saying so many different things or if there were some guarantee that parents have infallible wisdom.

Fortunately, such unreflective people are rare and most of us, through experience, have learned that things aren't always as they seem to be or as we want them to be. We are perplexed by so many different "explanations," given by so many authorities, of how the world works. We have come to realize that many of the things we have at one time accepted as true have been shown at some later time to be at odds with reality. Thus, we exercise due caution before accepting some claim as true, for we want good reasons or the right sort of evidence for it. For most of us, our picture of the world is a work-in-progress. We are continually taking in new data and restructuring our conceptual apparatus in order to accommodate this data in a consistent and coherent way. We have a critical attitude.

As is the case with any normative discipline, there are rules and guidelines for a correct approach to critical reasoning. This booklet attempts to introduce you to these rules in a manner that is friendly and informative. So-ooo . . .

3) LET'S GET CRITICAL!

There are a number of reasons for you to adopt a critical attitude and to use critical reasoning. I enumerate some below.

A) Internal Stability

A critical attitude helps you to strive for internal stability—that is, a type of mental solidity that is characterized (1) by proportioning conviction of belief to evidence and (2) by holding consistency in highest regard. Proportioning conviction of belief to the evidence on its behalf is, of course, a commitment toward trying to see the world as it really is instead of imposing your own structure or values on it. Holding consistency in greatest regard is a commitment to not readily accepting some claim as true if it conflicts with other claims that you have good grounds to believe are true.

B) Resolution of Conflict

Critical-reasoning skills are the best tools for resolution of conflict at any level. Critical reasoning is an appeal to reasons and evidence, not persuasion through force, bribery, fear, or emotion. It is therefore an essential tool for resolving tension within yourself, tension between yourself and others, and tension within and between groups of people—like religious factions, political parties, or nations.

C) Success in Attaining Goals

Critical-reasoning skills can be put to use in bettering personal decisions in an effort to reach your aims in life. Making decisions based on good reasons is always preferable to acting on a whim or acting according to someone else's advice, which may not be in your best interest. Deliberative calculation makes success at attaining goals much more likely than non-deliberative action. (Deliberative calculation also puts you in a better position to determine precisely what goals are the right goals to have in life!)

D) Open-Mindedness and Inquiry

A commitment to critical reasoning requires that you are open to rationally founded views that are inconsistent with your own. You assume fallibility and fallibility is a willingness to entertain all reasonable claims as true, if only provisionally, in an effort to increase understanding for all parties involved. Thus, a critical attitude is essentially one that is unselfish.

E) Fallibility and Open-Mindedness

Exposing a position to criticism enables you to gain the fullest possible understanding of its strengths and flaws. By knowing the flaws of your own position, for instance, you will be able to bolster this position through eliminating or, at least, addressing these flaws. If critical exposure shows your position to be untenable, then you will be able to escape error through greater understanding of your position (which is, as the ancient Greek poet Homer said, a "gold-for-bronze exchange").

F) Intellectual Integrity

Critical reasoning is a commitment to an honest search for truth, conceptual clarification, or heightened understanding. Reasoning skills, therefore, lead to personal growth through greater understanding of yourself and the world around you. Overall, demanding evidence before believing something to be true is not something to be reviled, but something of which you should be proud.

Module Three

On Reading Philosophy

1) GENERAL FORM OF A
PHILOSOPHICAL ESSAY OR BOOK

Since this is a booklet on critical reasoning and philosophy, the remarks in this module will focus on how to read philosophy with a critical eye. To this end, elements like philosophical creativity, enjoyment, and vision may get short shrift.

In the main, philosophical works take the form of elaborating on an existing philosophical problem or the discovery of a new problem.

A) Elaborating on an Existing Philosophical Problem

If the author is elaborating on an existing philosophical problem, follow these guidelines:

Try to find a clear statement of what the problem is. This should be spelled out early in the essay or book.

Look for this author's account of other estimable philosophical attempts to clear up the problem as well as arguments on why these attempts are unsuccessful or misdirected. This should follow the statement of the problem. (On existing problems, there is generally a good amount of literature and authors should make some mention of this literature.) Reference to this shows the extent to which this author is familiar with other literature on the problem. It also gives you as a reader some idea of the direction the author is taking in his attempted solution.

Look for an articulation of the author's own solution, and reasons why this solution is preferable to all others that have been proposed, if any do exist.

B) Disclosure of a New Philosophical Problem

If the author has discovered a new problem, follow these guidelines:

Look for solid arguments on behalf of why this problem is a genuine philosophical problem and not merely a pseudo-problem.
Examine these arguments closely. They need to be compelling. Genuine philosophical problems do not just spring up each and every day.
Look for an attempt to solve the problem in a latter part of the essay. In serious philosophical inquiry, however, disclosure of a new, genuine problem is certainly sufficient work in an essay or book. So, no solution may be given. The thesis should be helpful here.

2) THREE STEPS TO FOLLOW

A) Identify the Author's Thesis

Essays

This should come relatively early in the essay. The statement of thesis should always be written in such a way to make it clear to readers that it is the thesis statement. This, however, is not always the case, so be cautious.

Books

Read carefully the title, preface, introduction, and table of contents. These should make manifest the author's intent and main line of argument.

Tip: Underline or write out the thesis and any other statement that shows plainly the structure of the paper (or book) and its author's line of argument. Remember, often what an author intends to do is written out in several sentences.

Example (article in a journal):

> (1) Issues of social justice are among the most intellectually challenging
> to both the ethicist and philosopher of law, especially when there appear
> to be permanent, biologically determined differences of ability and po-
> tential among the people and between the groups for whom justice is
> sought. (2) Such is the case between men and women in the realm of
> sports. (3) The problem of providing justice in this area has been the topic
> of popular magazine articles, federal and state legislation, adjudication
> and philosophical contemplation. (4) But the heart of the matter has yet to
> be discussed. (5) I will attempt to do this [i.e. get at the heart of the mat-
> ter] by first reviewing some of the current issues in this area, (6) then ex-
> ploring the relationship between the use and exchange values of athletic
> participation, and (7) finally proposing a radical solution which is de-
> fended on utilitarian, egalitarian and Rawlsian ethical grounds. (8) The re-
> sult will be an approach to promoting social justice and equality amongst
> biologically diverse groups which may be applicable beyond the area of
> sports. (Kathryn Pyne Addelson, "Equality and Competition: Can Sports
> Make a Woman of a Girl?")

Analysis:

1) Statements one through four set up the problem: gender equality in
   sports. Statement four indicates that all attempts to solve this problem have missed the crux of the matter.
2) Statements five through eight indicate in a clear and systematic manner just what this author proposes to do in her paper, though no precise
   articulation of a thesis is contained within these final four statements.

B) Look for Arguments in Support of the Thesis

Essays

Look at the overall structure of a paper for support of the thesis. Good
writers will use their thesis and introductory paragraph as a guide to the
format of the remainder of their paper. For instance, if the thesis is compound, each of the sections of the paper may represent one of the components of the thesis (though this need not be the case). Arguments on
behalf of the thesis, however, can be contained in one or many sections
of the paper.

Books

Look to the table of contents for guidance. This is in a straightforward sense an author's outline of the book's content. Different chapters can contain different arguments for a thesis or, as the case with essays, all arguments can come in one chapter or a few.

Tip: Beginning with the thesis, make a general outline of the paper or book. (For the latter, be content with a broad outline.) Next, fill in your outline by fleshing out each of the main arguments with a second or third reading (or more, if necessary).

C) Evaluation of Arguments on Behalf of Thesis

The final step for reading philosophy concerns critical analysis of the arguments given on its behalf. This requires much more discussion that I can give in this module. I shall discuss this fully in the third section of modules. For now, be content with being sure that you have faithfully captured an author's main line of argument.

Tip: Don't be frustrated if you fail to grasp what an author is getting at in a single reading or even in a few readings. Philosophical works are often very dense and rich. One suggestion is to settle first for a comfortable feel for what is being argued, and then reread the work in an effort to flesh out precisely the line of argument. Multiple readings of philosophical works are generally necessary (even for professional philosophers). Don't be frustrated by the time and effort this takes, for your aim is a full understanding and this, you will find, is its own reward. Critical analysis of philosophical material, like any other skill, takes practice to develop and practice takes time. Most important, expect to make numerous mistakes along the way. Ask your instructor for help, if necessary.

Section Two

ARGUMENT RECOGNITION AND RECONSTRUCTION

Module Four

The Elements of Analysis

1) SENTENCES VS. STATEMENTS

A) What Is a Sentence?

A sentence *is a unit of communication in a given language—a syntactic conjunction of words that is grammatically sound according to the rules of that language.*

Examples of proper sentences:

1) Roxanne likes to hike.
2) Is the wizard really a good wizard?
3) Get yourself ready for dinner!
4) Try the Teriyaki Chicken.

Of these, each is a grammatically sound string of words in English and each communicates something that is readily accessible to another English-speaking person. The first is a *declarative sentence* in that it admits of truth or falsity. The second is a *question*. The third is an *order*. The last is a *suggestion*.

Examples of improper sentences:

1) Roxanne likes to hike to.
2) Wizard really good?
3) Yourself for ready get dinner!
4) The Teriyaki try Chicken.

Each of these has at least one flaw. The first ends in a preposition ("to" . . .) that has no object. The second example lacks a verb. The third and fourth have all the components for a sentence, but the ordering violates proper English syntax.

B) What Is a Statement?

A statement *is the meaning or truth-value of a declarative sentence.*

Like all declarative sentences, every statement admits of truth or falsity in that it asserts something is the case (rightly or wrongly).

Examples:

1) The 5:15 train is running on time.
2) Alexander's cat was hit by a car.
3) The tenor's voice was flat last night.

As a statement is really the propositional content of a declarative sentence, I shall use the words "statement" and "proposition" as synonymous throughout.

C) Statement/Sentence Distinction

Different sentences can have the same propositional content.

Examples:

1) I love a good stout.
2) A good stout is loved by me.

Here there are two dissimilar declarative sentences that assert exactly the same thing and thus mean the same thing. Having the same meaning translates into being the same statement.

The same sentence can have different propositional content.

I am the most miserly person alive.

Consider how the meaning of this changes when it is uttered by different people. Consider also the same sentence with "I," "most," or "miserly" emphasized.

A sentence can contain more than one (simple) proposition.

Example:

> The Countess Laia lost her diamond earrings, but she found them several days later.

This single sentence is really a conjunction of two statements that are separated by a comma and the word "but." Thus it makes two separate claims: "The countess lost her diamond earrings" and "She [the countess] found them several days later."

All propositions are either true or false, while this is not the case for all sentences (only declarative sentences).

Examples:

1) Command: Catch the bus!
2) Proposal: Let's go to the ballpark today.
3) Question: Who is the best fashion designer in all of Europe?
4) Exclamation: Radical, dude!
5) Suggestion: I suggest you take the ferry.
6) Declarative Sentence: Zoltan bought a new car yesterday.

Of these, only example six is making a statement and, consequently, is a proposition. In other words, only the last admits of truth or falsity.

Note: Certain questions, *rhetorical questions*, have a function in language that is not interrogatory, but instead declarative. Therefore, rhetorical questions are really not questions at all, but assertions.

Example:

> "Is your finger on the frosting of your sister's birthday cake?" (said to a boy who has his finger on his sister's birthday cake)

Since it is clear that this question is not a request for an answer, it is better understood as an assertion, "I see that your finger is on your sister's birthday cake," or possibly a command, "Get your finger off your sister's birthday cake!" Context will help determine whether or not it is a proposition that forms part of an argument.

2) WHAT IS AN ARGUMENT?

A) Arguments and Their Parts

Arguments are commonly understood as verbal disputes between parties, often ones that are heated, where each is trying to convince the other of the truth of some point. In such exchanges, the methods of persuasion are virtually limitless. One party may choose reasons, force, pity, or even trickery to get a point through.

For purposes of critical reasoning, this is both too narrow, in one sense, and too broad, in another. It is too narrow, as we shall see, in that persuasion is merely one of the aims of critical reasoning. It is too broad in that, when persuasion is the aim, the means of persuasion must not be rhetorical, but based exclusively on evidence or reasons.

Preliminary Definitions:

An argument *is a collection of propositions whereby evidence in the form of at least one proposition (the premise) is given in support of another proposition (the conclusion).*

A premise *is a proposition that is given as evidence for another proposition in an argument.*

The conclusion *is a proposition that purportedly follows from the evidence in an argument.*

Example:

[1]There must be some gas left in the tank. [2]I filled the tank last night.

Here proposition one (the conclusion) purportedly follows from proposition two (the premise), which is given as evidence for proposition one. The relationship between premise(s) and the conclusion can be depicted as follows:

Premise(s)
(**P** justifies **C**)
↓
Conclusion
(**C** is justified by **P**)

Often, several premises are given on behalf of a single conclusion. These premises can function independently of each other (where two or more premises work apart from each other and form separate arguments on behalf of the conclusion) or dependently (where two or more premises work together to attempt to justify the conclusion), or there can be some combination of both at play. In summary, premises are put forth in order to justify a conclusion—that is, to show that it is true—while the conclusion in the right sort of argument is justified by the premises.

As we shall see in subsequent modules, arguments are often compound—comprising many smaller arguments within a large, complex argument.

B) Two Reasons that We Argue

We give arguments in an attempt to persuade others of the truth of some statement through an appeal to evidence and reasons in support of that statement, not appeals to pity, slander, or force.

Examples:

1) [1]Norbert must have committed the crime, [2]since he is a mean-spirited rogue.
2) [1]Norbert must have committed the crime, since [2]he is the owner of the murder weapon and [3]he was at the scene of the crime when the murder occurred.

Example two purports to provide the sort of evidence for the conclusion, "Norbert must have committed the crime," that is rationally compelling, while example one tries to persuade by what is likely an unjustifiable slander against an agent. This is not to say that the first example is not an argument. It is an argument, but a very bad one.

Arguments can extend our knowledge of things in ways that are not initially obvious.

Here persuasion may not be relevant at all. One may, for example, simply be drawing out the consequences of some statement in a manner that discloses new information (though information that was there implicitly all the while).

Examples:

1) In an infinite universe, every point can be regarded as the center, because every point has an infinite number of stars on each side of it. (Stephen Hawking, *A Brief History of Time*)
2) Rhonda weighs more than Cindy and Cindy weighs more than Felix, so Rhonda weighs more than Felix.

In both examples, the conclusions (underlined) may not at all be obvious without the evidence of the premises.

C) Conditions of Acceptance

We can summarize everything we've said about arguments below:

The function of an argument *is to establish the truth of its conclusion by means of asserting as true at least one other proposition (the premise).*

Note: Asserting something to be true is no guarantee that what is being asserted is true.

Overall, two conditions must be met before anyone is in a position to accept a conclusion as true. Let us call these the *conditions of acceptance*:

CA₁: All of the premises of an argument must be true (i.e., what is asserted as true in the premises actually is true).

CA₂: The premises, assumed true, must provide absolute support (generally called "deductively validity") or an appropriate degree of support (generally called "inductively strength") for the conclusion.

When either of these two principles has not been met, there is good reason *not* to accept the conclusion as true (though it still may be true). When the second condition is violated, we have a fallacy.

A fallacy *is an argument in which the premises purport to but do not provide adequate support for the conclusion.*

A more detailed analysis of the function of arguments and fallacies comes later. For now, the aim has been simply to give you a general feel for what an argument is and to define some of the most fundamental terms that we shall be using throughout.

Module Five

Ten Helpful Steps

In this module, I list ten steps that will provide assistance in recognizing and reconstructing arguments. Recognition is vital for the obvious reason that analysis of an argument cannot proceed without it. Reconstruction is vital in that no critical analysis of an argument can take place without a precise grasp of just what the argument is stating.

1) LOOK FOR AND CIRCLE ALL REASONING INDICATORS IN A PASSAGE YOU SUSPECT CONTAINS AN ARGUMENT.

Reasoning indicators are words that may function to designate a statement that follows as a premise or conclusion of an argument. Here is a fairly complete list of premise and conclusion indicators.

Premise indicators:

> because, since, for, for the reason that, given that, on account of, assuming that, follows from, supposing, may be inferred from, may be deduced from, as derived from, owing to, seeing that, as, inasmuch as, as shown by, in view of the fact that, as indicated by

Conclusion indicators:

> therefore, thus, it follows that, hence, so, implies, entails that, suggests that, demonstrates that, shows, accordingly, is a reason for, this is why, conse-

quently, as a result, proves that, which shows that, for this reason (looks like a premise indicator, but "this" points backward)

If a word is a reasoning indicator, it will function *exclusively* as a premise or a conclusion indicator; no one word has both functions in the English language. However, some words that function as reasoning indicators have other meanings also. "Thus," when it is used as a reasoning indicator, will always designate a conclusion (meaning "therefore"). But "thus" can also function adverbially (meaning "in this manner"), and this does not designate a conclusion. "Since" can be a premise indicator or it can merely indicate the passing of time. So, reasoning indicators should not be used as infallible guides.

Examples:

1) Annette likes to think,(thus)she will probably become a philosopher.
2) Ajax ran the race with intrepidity,(thus)he wore out the soles of his shoes.

"Thus" functions as a conclusion indicator only in the first set of statements for there is really nothing being argued for in the second. (A clear explanation of this comes with step five.)

Examples:

1) (Since)Annette likes to think, she will probably become a philosopher.

2) (Since)Roxanne left, Alexander was sad.

"Since" in the last set of statements merely marks the passing of time. In the first, it picks out a premise.

2) NUMBER ALL THE STATEMENTS IN THE PASSAGE THAT YOU SUSPECT CONTAINS AN ARGUMENT.

Example:

The habit of viewing life as a whole is an essential part both of wisdom and of true morality, and is one of the things which ought to be encouraged in education. Consistent purpose is not enough to make life happy, but it is an almost indispensable condition of a happy life. And consistent purpose embodies itself mainly in work. (Bertrand Russell, *Conquest of Happiness*)

With numbers:

> [1]The habit of viewing life as a whole is an essential part both of wisdom and of true morality, and [2]is one of the things which ought to be encouraged in education. [3]Consistent purpose is not enough to make life happy, but [4]it is an almost indispensable condition of a happy life. And [5]consistent purpose embodies itself mainly in work.

Note: Here the first two sentences contain two statements that are linked by a conjunctive word ("and," "but," "yet," etc.). A conjunctive word is one whose function is just to link together different statements. I go into greater detail in module seven.

3) AMONG THESE STATEMENTS, CHECK TO SEE WHETHER THERE IS ONE STATEMENT IN PARTICULAR THAT REQUIRES SUPPORT. IF SO, UNDERLINE IT.

Example:

> [1]Utopian social engineering is fundamentally in conflict with the complexity of the human condition, and [2]social creativity blossoms best when political power is restrained. That basic lesson makes it all the more likely that [3]democracy—and not communism—will dominate the twenty-first century. (Zbigniew Brzezinski, *The Grand Failure*)

All of these statements are contentious. Yet statements one and two here work together as evidence for the third proposition, which really begins after the phrase "that basic lesson makes it all the more likely that . . ." (which itself functions as a lengthy conclusion indicator).

With conclusion underlined:

> [1]Utopian social engineering is fundamentally in conflict with the complexity of the human condition, and [2]social creativity blossoms best when political power is restrained. That basic lesson makes it all the more likely that <u>[3]democracy—and not communism—will dominate the twenty-first century.</u>

4) IF YOU FIND A STATEMENT IN NEED OF SUPPORT, LOOK FOR AT LEAST ONE OTHER STATEMENT PURPORTING TO PROVIDE SUCH SUPPORT.

Examples:

1) [1]There was a huge sex scandal at the college. [2]The chancellor will be fired shortly. [3]The women's basketball team lost its 12th straight game.
2) [1]There was a huge sex scandal at the college. [2]The chancellor is suspected to be the main person involved in it. [3]The chancellor will be fired shortly.

There are three statements in each example, some of which are statements that could function as a conclusion of an argument. However, only in the second example is there a statement that is contentious, "The chancellor will be fired shortly," that is given support (the first two propositions). In example one, there is nothing to link any of the three statements together in the form of an argument. So, we likely have three distinct and unrelated statements.

Analysis of example two:

[1]There was a huge sex scandal at the college. [2]The chancellor is suspected to be the main person involved in it. [3]The chancellor will be fired shortly.

Problem: What if you know that two statements make up an argument but have difficulty in distinguishing premise from conclusion?

Example[1]:

[1]There is nothing circular about classifying events in terms of their effects; [2]the criterion is both empirical and objective. (B. F. Skinner, *Science and Human Behavior*)

Example[2]:

[1]Men are never convinced of your reasons, of your sincerity, of the seriousness of your sufferings, except by your death. [2]So long as you are alive, your case is doubtful; you have a right only to your skepticism. (Albert Camus, *The Fall*)

In both examples, you may intuitively know that there is an argument, but not know which proposition is the premise and which is the conclusion. In such cases, use the *principle of alternation* as a guide.

If you cannot decide which of two statements is the conclusion try the first as the premise and the second as the conclusion and see whether this makes sense; if this does not make sense, try the second as the premise and the first as the conclusion.

Analysis₁:

> ¹There is nothing circular about classifying events in terms of their ef-
> fects; ²the criterion is both empirical and objective.

Here statement one is a consequence of statement two.

Analysis₂:

> ¹Men are never convinced of your reasons, of your sincerity, of the seri-
> ousness of your sufferings, except by your death. ²So long as you are
> alive, your case is doubtful; you have a right only to your skepticism.

The *principle of alternation* makes it clear that statement one is the conclusion of example one and statement two is the conclusion of example two.

5) UPON FINDING THE STATEMENT PUTATIVELY NEEDING SUPPORT (A POSSIBLE CONCLUSION TO AN ARGUMENT), ASK YOURSELF WHETHER THIS STATEMENT IS BEST TAKEN AS FACTUAL OR AS A STATEMENT IN NEED OF JUSTIFICATION.

If it is best taken as factual, then it is likely that there is no argument. If not, then it is likely that there is an argument.

Examples:

1) ¹The house burned down, because ² Olga was smoking in her bed.

2) ¹The house will burn down, because ²Olga constantly smokes in her bed.

In example one, it would be improper to take "because" as a reasoning indicator (premise indicator), since the truth of the statement, "The house burned down," is not in question. This statement is factual and needs no *justification*, but it does ask to be *explained*. In other words, its truth is not in question, but its cause is. So, this is not an argument, but an *explanation*.

In this second example, "because" functions to introduce a premise for the statement, "The house will burn down." The future-directedness of this statement gives no doubt about it being in need of justification here.

Note: Certain seeming premise indicators, especially the word "because," can designate an argument or an explanation. So, when something appears to be an argument, ask yourself if the would-be conclusion is in question or not. Follow the *principle of discernment*.

If the would-be conclusion of something that appears to be an argument is plainly factual, there is no argument, but an explanation.

Problem: There are cases where it is not possible to know whether a statement is indeed factual or otherwise.

Example:

¹Bohdan looks old, because ²his wife has passed away.

Here "Bohdan looks old" may be factual or not, depending upon whether *in fact* he really does look old. With no context to help, it seems impossible to state plainly whether or not this is an argument.

6) PUT ALL STATEMENTS INTO THEIR SIMPLEST AND CLEAREST FORM.

Example:

¹If a sleeping person could note that it is raining or judge that his wife is jealous, then why could he not judge that he is asleep? ²The absurdity of the latter proves the absurdity of the former. (Norman Malcolm, *Dreaming*)

This is a difficult argument to reconstruct. The first statement is rhetorical. It can and should be rewritten thus: "If a sleeping person could note that it is raining or judge that his wife is jealous, then he would be able to judge that he is asleep." In doing so, we find the latter sentence to be really making two statements that have reference to each of the two parts of first sentence, which is a conditional (an if-then statement). The reworked argument looks something like this:

> [1]If a sleeping person could note that it is raining or judge that his wife is jealous, then he would be able to judge that he is asleep. Yet [2]he cannot judge that he is asleep, ⓈⓄ [3]he cannot judge that it is raining or that his wife is jealous.

7) CHECK WHETHER THERE ARE PARTS OF THE ARGUMENT LEFT UNSTATED AND FILL THESE IN ACCORDINGLY.

Example:

> [1]Noble and beautiful works of art should not be subjected to haste; and [2]this majestic new world is indeed a most noble and beautiful work. (Mark Twain, *The Diary of Adam and Eve*)

What is implicitly concluded here is the statement, "This majestic new world should not be subjected to haste." It is thought so obvious that it need not be explicitly stated. Fill this in, however.

> [1]Noble and beautiful works of art should not be subjected to haste; and [2]this majestic new world is indeed a most noble and beautiful work. [So, [3]this majestic new world should not be subjected to haste.]

8) ELIMINATE IRRELEVANT STATEMENTS.

Example₁:

> Ⓐⓢ [1]there is nothing fundamentally new to be offered in this field since the researches of Freud, Adler, and Stekel, [2]we must content ourselves with corroborating their experiences by citing parallel cases. [3]I have un-

der observation a few cases of this kind which may be worth reporting for their general interest. (C. G. Jung, "On the Significance of Number Dreams")

Here, the second statement is the conclusion and the first gives evidence on its behalf. The third statement does nothing to establish the conclusion's truth; it merely indicates to readers that Jung is about to offer three instances of number dreams that corroborate the work of Freud, Adler, and Stekel. So, strike out the final statement.

(As) [1]there is nothing fundamentally new to be offered in this field since the researches of Freud, Adler, and Stekel, [2]we must content ourselves with corroborating their experiences by citing parallel cases. [3]I have under observation a few cases of this kind which may be worth reporting for their general interest. (C. G. Jung, "On the Significance of Number Dreams")

Example$_2$:

[1]There is no respect for the views of others as truth or partial truth; [2]they are from the beginning treated as diseases, sources of vulnerability to disturbance; and [3]the aim [of Skepticism] from the beginning is to subvert them, knock them out. This is so not because, as in Epicureanism, the teacher statements to have the truth already — but because truth is not sought, from any source. (Martha Nussbaum, *The Therapy of Desire*)

In this passage, statement four is asserted as something that is *not* a reason for what is concluded. Only the fifth is given as evidence. Yet this statement could equally be seen as evidence for each of the first three statements. Are the first three statements put forth as three conclusions with statement five as support? It is conceivable that they are. Nussbaum's use of "This is so," however, suggests that only the third statement is the conclusion—otherwise she would probably have begun the second sentence as "These are so. . . ."

[1]There is no respect for the views of others as truth or partial truth; [2]they are from the beginning treated as diseases, sources of vulnerability to disturbance; and [3]the aim [of Skepticism] from the beginning is to subvert them, knock them out. This is so not because, [4]as in Epicureanism, the teacher statements to have the truth already — but (because) [5]truth is not sought, from any source. (Martha Nussbaum, *The Therapy of Desire*)

9) WRITE OUT THE ENTIRE
ARGUMENT IN STANDARD FORM.

This is a very important step, especially if you desire to have the best conceivable grasp of an argument.

Guidelines for standard form:

Number all statements and order them as follows: Place premises first, then place the conclusion last (prefacing it by the word "so").
Use brackets [ ] for implicit statements.
Strike out any irrelevant statements.
After each conclusion, place numbers in parentheses to indicate how it was derived.

Example$_1$:

> ¹Noble and beautiful works of art should not be subjected to haste; and ²this majestic new world is indeed a most noble and beautiful work. [So, ³this majestic new world should not be subjected to haste.]

Standard form:

1) Noble and beautiful works of art should not be subjected to haste.
2) This majestic new world is indeed a most noble and beautiful work.
3) [So, this majestic new world should not be subjected to haste.]
   (1 & 2)

Here the conclusion, bracketed, is not explicit, but implicit.

Example$_2$:

> ¹If it is the nature of the earth as a whole to float on water, the same should be true of every piece of it; but ²this is plainly contrary to fact, for ³a piece taken at random sinks to the bottom, and ⁴the larger it is the quicker it sinks. (Aristotle, *On the Heavens*)

Standard form:

1) If it is the nature of the earth as a whole to float on water, the same should be true of every piece of it.
3) Any random piece sinks to the bottom of water.
2) So, it is not the nature of earth to float on water (1 & 3).

Statement one is a conditional (an "if-then" statement) that should not be broken into separate statements (see module seven). Also, statement two is not the denial of the whole of statement one, but it implicitly denies only the antecedent or "if" part of it. Statement four adds interesting information about the *rate* of fall for earth in water, but this is not relevant for establishing the truth of the conclusion.

Example$_3$:

> [1]If you quarrel with all your sense-perceptions you will have nothing to refer to in judging even those sense-perceptions which you statement are false. (Epicurus, *Principle Doctrines*)

Strictly speaking, this is no argument, since it is only one statement—a lengthy conditional statement—and for there to be an argument there must be at least two statements. Yet it seems clear that this should be taken as an argument, which can be fleshed out as follows.

Standard form:

1) If you quarrel with all your sense-perceptions you will have nothing to refer to in judging even those sense-perceptions which you statement are false.
2) [There must be some standard of judgment for sense-perceptions.]
3) [So, no one can quarrel with all sense-impressions.] (1 & 2)

10) WHEN YOU'VE COMPLETED THE PRIOR STEPS, READ THE ARGUMENT THROUGH CAREFULLY AS A FINAL CHECK TO YOUR RECONSTRUCTION.

Section Three

DIAGRAMMING ARGUMENTS

Module Six

Fundamentals of Diagramming

1) TWO TYPES OF ARGUMENT

A) Simple Arguments

A simple argument *is one that is uncompounded—that is, it has only one evidential link (one arrow).*

Examples:

1) Sandeep loves to travel, as he has a brand new set of suitcases in his basement.
2) Alexander loves to travel, as he does so often and what he does often, he loves.

Analyses:

1) ¹Sandeep loves to travel, as ²he has a brand new set of suitcases in his basement.
2) ¹Alexander loves to travel, as ²he does so often and ³what he does often, he loves.

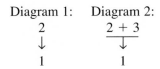

Diagram 1:   Diagram 2:
2   2 + 3
↓   ↓
1   1

B) Compound Arguments

A compound argument *is an argument with more than one evidential link (one arrow).*

Examples (these are fairly tough, though they serve the purpose of illustration):

1) Self-interest, or rather self-love, or *egoism*, has been more plausibly substituted as the basis of morality. But I consider our relations with others as constituting the boundaries of morality. With ourselves, we stand on the ground of identity, not of relation, which last, requiring two subjects, excludes self-love confined to a single one. To ourselves, in strict language, we can owe no duties, obligation requiring also two parties. Self-love, therefore, is no part of morality. (Thomas Jefferson to Thomas Law, 1814. *ME* 14:140)

2) As we continually see that organisms of all kinds are rendered in some degree sterile from their constitutions having been disturbed by slightly different and new conditions of life, we need not feel surprise at hybrids being in some degree sterile, for their constitutions can hardly fail to have been disturbed from being compounded of two distinct organisations. This parallelism is supported by another parallel, but directly opposite, class of facts; namely, that the vigour and fertility of all organic beings are increased by slight changes in their conditions of life, and that the offspring of slightly modified forms or varieties acquire from being crossed increased vigour and fertility. So that, on the one hand, considerable changes in the conditions of life and crosses between greatly modified forms, lessen fertility; and on the other hand, lesser changes in the conditions of life and crosses between less modified forms, increase fertility. (Charles Darwin, *Origin of Species*)

Analyses:

1) [1]~~Self-interest, or rather self-love, or *egoism*, has been more plausibly substituted as the basis of morality.~~ But [2]I consider our relations with others as constituting the boundaries of morality. [3]With ourselves, we stand on the ground of identity, not of relation, which last, requiring two subjects, excludes self-love confined to a single one. [4]To ourselves, in strict language, we <u>can owe no duties</u>, obligation requiring also two parties. [5]Self-love, (therefore), is <u>no part of morality</u>.

2) (As) we continually see that ¹organisms of all kinds are rendered in
some degree sterile from their constitutions having been disturbed by
slightly different and new conditions of life, we need not feel surprise
at ²hybrids being in some degree sterile, (for) ³their constitutions can
hardly fail to have been disturbed from being compounded of two distinct organisations. ⁴~~This parallelism is supported by another parallel,
but directly opposite, class of facts~~; namely, that ⁵the vigour and fertility of all organic beings are increased by slight changes in their conditions of life, and that ⁶the offspring of slightly modified forms or varieties acquire from being crossed increased vigour and fertility. (So)
that, on the one hand, ⁷considerable changes in the conditions of life
and crosses between greatly modified forms, lessen fertility; and on
the other hand, ⁸lesser changes in the conditions of life and crosses between less modified forms, increase fertility.

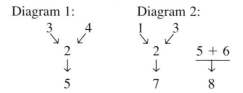

Diagram 1:   Diagram 2:

The second compound argument is really two arguments, since the conclusion is two separate statements supported by different chunks of evidence. Most of the arguments we'll be analyzing will be like these two
examples.

2) MULTIPLE REASONS

Often, two or more premises are given for the same conclusion. Here
we must decide whether these premises work together to support the
conclusion (i.e., they are dependent) or they work separately (i.e., they
are independent).

A) Dependent Reasons

Premises are called dependent *when they must be taken together in support of a conclusion.*

Example:

> The fish Delphina purchased are foul, since all of the fish at Smedley's
> Market are foul and Delphina purchased her fish there.

Analysis:

> [1]The fish Delphina purchased are foul, (since) [2]all of the fish at Smedley's
> Market are foul and [3]Delphina purchased her fish there.

Diagrammed:

$$\frac{2 + 3}{\downarrow}$$
$$1$$

B) Independent Reasons

Premises are called independent *when each is a separate reason in support of a conclusion.*

Example:

> The fish Delphina purchased are foul, since they had a bad smell when
> she bought them and she left them out on the counter overnight.

Analysis:

> [1]The fish Delphina purchased are foul, (since) [2]she they had a bad smell
> when she bought them and [3]she left them out on the counter overnight.

Diagrammed:

$$2 \quad 3$$
$$\searrow \quad \swarrow$$
$$1$$

3) DUAL CONCLUSIONS

A premise can support more than one conclusion, yet this is rare.

Example:

> Titormus hoisted the massive, 200-kilogram boulder from the earth. So, he'll be exhausted this evening and the frustration of failing to lift it before is over.

Analysis:

> [1]Titormus hoisted the massive, 200-kilogram boulder from the earth. So, [2]he'll be exhausted this evening and [3]his frustration from failing to lift it before is over.

Diagrammed:

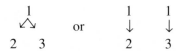

Note: Both diagrammatical representations are the same. Each says that statement one is given in support of statements two and three. The links from one to two and one to three must be assessed independently of each other.

Module Seven

Ten Diagrammatical Tips

1) DO NOT BREAK CONDITIONAL SENTENCES INTO SEPARATE STATEMENTS.

A *conditional* (if-then) sentence functions as a single statement that asserts a special relationship between its antecedent (the "if" part) and consequent (the "then" part): It asserts that the truth of the antecedent is sufficient to guarantee the truth of the consequent—not that its antecedent or its consequent is true. This link between antecedent and consequent is not evidentiary, however, so conditionals are not arguments, though a conditional can be a premise or a conclusion of one. As such a conditional is a compound statement whose separate parts, because of the function of if-then statements, do *not* make separate statements.

Example:

If *The Village of Stepanchikovo* was written by Dostoyevsky, then it could not have been written as satire.

Here neither "*The Village of Stepanchikovo* was written by Dostoyevsky" nor "It could not have been written as satire" are being asserted as true. What is being asserted is that the truth of the antecedent is sufficient to guarantee the truth of the consequent.

Schematically:

Antecedent | is sufficient for ⟩ **Consequent**

Some words indicative of conditionals:

> if, if . . . then, when(ever), is contingent upon, is necessary for, is suffi-cient for, unless (if not), only if, provided that, on condition that.

Standard form:

> If I don't get a job, then I'll go hungry.

Alternative forms:

> Going hungry *is contingent upon* not getting a job.
> I'll go hungry *unless* I get a job.
> *Whenever* I don't get a job, I go hungry.
> Not getting a job *is sufficient for* going hungry.
> Going hungry *is necessary for* not getting a job.
> I don't get a job *only if* I go hungry.
> *Provided that* I don't get a job, I'll go hungry.
> I'll go hungry *on condition that* I don't get a job.

2) A SENTENCE WHOSE MAJOR CONNECTIVE IS "OR" IS ONE STATEMENT.

Example:

> [1]*Alexander will become president of the Elks Club or he'll quit the Elks.*

Although there are two separate statements here, the word "or" func-tions in language in such a manner that the whole sentence makes one statement. In effect, it asserts that the whole sentence is true if *at least one* of the disjunctive parts is true.

3) BREAK UP A SENTENCE WHOSE MAJOR CONNECTIVE IS "AND."

Example[1]:

> [1]Roxanne went to the dance and [2]she drank too much wine.

The word "and" functions such that, when it is the primary connective in a sentence, that sentence is true *only when all* of the conjunctive parts are true. In short, each conjunctive part makes a separate statement.

Example$_2$:

[1]Roxanne and Alexander went to the dance.

Though there are literally two statements her—"Roxanne went to the dance" and "Alexander went to the dance"—convenience suggests there is no need to break up conjunctive statements like this one.

4) LEARN TO IDENTIFY THE MAJOR CONNECTIVE ("AND," "OR," "IF . . . THEN," AND "NOT") OF A LARGE STATEMENT.

Examples:

1) Whenever Janine finds herself with nothing to do, she gets antsy and she puts on some jazz.
2) Either Courtney will get some tea and Felicia will get a sandwich or Andy will get himself a beer.
3) Both Rodney ran the race in splendid time or Wilma gets angry and Rodney did not run the race in splendid time.
4) Bambi will not sing unless she is fitfully paid, and she is not fitfully paid.
5) Either the failed arrival of Embricia's exercise machine is sufficient for her being upset or she will do some yoga.

Analyses:

1) A conditional whose consequent is a conjunction.
   Whenever Janine finds herself with nothing to do, [she gets antsy *and* she puts on some jazz].
2) This could be either a conjunctive or a disjunctive statement, but the word "either" tells us that it is a disjunction whose first disjunctive part is a conjunction.
   Either [Courtney will get some tea *and* Felicia will get a sandwich] *or* Andy will get himself a beer.
3) The word "both" disambiguates this sentence as a conjunctive statement.

Both [Rodney ran the race in splendid time *or* Wilma gets angry] *and* Rodney did *not* run the race in splendid time.

4) This could be a conditional or a conjunction. The comma after "paid" shows that it is a conjunction.
[Bambi will *not* sing *unless* she is fitfully paid], *and* she is *not* fitfully paid.

5) Again the word "either" is the key to disentangling the sentence.
Either [The failed arrival of Embricia's exercise machine *is sufficient for* her being upset] *or* she will do some yoga.

Note: In every example, lack of *disambiguators* (key words or suitable punctuation) would make it impossible to decide what the major connective of a sentence is. For instance, without the word "either" in example two, the sentence is ambiguous (i.e., it is impossible to tell whether it is a conjunction or a disjunction).

5) BE CAUTIOUS OF WORDS WITH CONCESSIVE FORCE (E.G., "BUT," "YET," "ALTHOUGH"). IN MANY CASES, WHAT IS BEING CONCEDED IS IRRELEVANT TO THE ARGUMENT.

Example$_1$:

Although¹you want to be at the convention, ²you will not, for ³you do not have the money for travel and ⁴you will not be able to take time off from work to attend.

Statement one, "you want to be at the convention," which follows the concessive word "although" (boxed), is irrelevant to establishing "you will not [be at the convention]" as true. Simply omit it from consideration.

Diagrammed:

3   4
↘ ↙
2

Example₂:

¹Now to ask whether it is reasonable to believe in scientific conclusions comes right down to asking whether one ought to fashion his beliefs on the basis of the available evidence. But ²this is what it means to be rational. Hence, ³the question amounts to asking whether it is rational to be rational. (Wesley Salmon, "An Encounter with David Hume")

Here the concessive statement, statement two, *is* relevant to the argument, for we cannot justify the conclusion without statements one and two.

Diagrammed:

$$\frac{1 + 2}{\downarrow}$$
$$3$$

Example₃:

¹Moderation in the affections and passions, self-control, and calm deliberation are not only good in many respects, but ²even seem to constitute part of the intrinsic worth of the person; but ³they are far from deserving to be called good without qualification, although ⁴they have been so unconditionally praised by the ancients. For ⁵without the principles of a good will, they may become extremely bad, and the ⁶coolness of a villain not only makes him far more dangerous, but ⁷also directly makes him more abominable in our eyes than he would have been without it. (Immanuel Kant, *Grounding for the Metaphysics of Morals*)

Diagrammed:

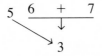

In this dense bit of text, there are four separate concessive words, each boxed. The second "but" functions to eliminate everything before it as part of the argument. What follows is the conclusion. What follows "although" is also irrelevant. The final concessive statement, statement seven, is however relevant to the conclusion.

6) THE WORD "AND" GENERALLY INDICATES THAT EACH OF THE CONJUNCTIVE STATEMENTS THAT ARE LINKED COME TO PLAY AT THE SAME LEVEL IN THE DIAGRAM.

Example:

> [1]Older people and sour people do not appear to be prone to friendship. (For) [2]there is little pleasure to be found in them and [3]no one can spend his days with what is painful or not pleasant, (since) [4]nature appears to avoid above all what is painful and to aim at what is pleasant. (Aristotle, *Nicomachean Ethics*)

The word "and" is not a reasoning indicator, but here it tells us that statements two and three are at the same level in the diagram—either they can be taken as dependent reasons for the conclusion or they can be independent reasons for the conclusion. They are dependent reasons.

Diagrammed:

$$
\begin{array}{c}
4 \\
\downarrow \\
2 \quad + \quad 3 \\
\hline
\downarrow \\
1
\end{array}
$$

7) IN THE MAIN, KEEP EXAMPLES OUT OF THE ARGUMENT. MOST OFTEN THEY SERVE TO ILLUSTRATE A CERTAIN POINT WITHOUT JUSTIFYING THAT POINT.

Example:

> [1]Remember that no matter what nature may have produced or may be producing, the means must necessarily have been adequate, must have been *fitted to that production.* [2]The argument from fitness to design would (consequently) always apply, whatever were the product's charac-ter. [3]The recent Mont-Pelée eruption, for example, required all previ-ous history to produce that exact combination of ruined houses, human and animal corpses, sunken ships, volcanic ashes, etc., in just that one

hideous configuration of positions. (William James, *Pragmatism—A New Name for Some Old Ways of Thinking*)

The third statement functions merely as an illustration of the point being made, not a justification of it. Simply omit it.

Diagrammed:

$$1$$
$$\downarrow$$
$$2$$

8) IF TWO STATEMENTS SAY THE SAME THING, LEAVE ONE OF THEM OUT OF THE DIAGRAM.

Example:

[1]Coherence alone is not enough for justification because [2]a coherent set of propositions may not be grounded in reality. [3]A fairy tale may be coherent, but that doesn't justify our believing it. Since [4]justification is supposed to be a reliable guide to the truth, and since [5]truth is grounded in reality, [6]there must be more to justification than mere coherence. (Schick and Vaughn, *How to Think about Weird Things*)

Here statement two justifies statement one and statement three functions merely as an illustration of statement two. Leave out statement three. Statements four and five justify statement six. However, statements one and six say precisely the same thing, so you can leave one of these out—say, statement one. Now, we are left with statements two, four, five, and six. If statement two justifies statement one and statements one and six are equivalent, then use statement two to justify statement six. But statement two can be left out if it says nothing more than what statements four and five say. It doesn't however, but it provides additional important information. We are left with statements two, four, and five justifying statements six dependently.

[1]~~Coherence alone is not enough for justification~~ because [2]a coherent set of propositions may not be grounded in reality. [3]~~A fairy tale may be coherent, but that doesn't justify our believing it.~~ Since [4]justification is

supposed to be a reliable guide to the truth, and (since) [5]truth is grounded in reality, [6]there must be more to justification than mere coherence.

Diagrammed:

$$2 \ + \ 4 \ + \ 5$$
$$\downarrow$$
$$6$$

9) DO NOT BREAK APART A SENTENCE WITH THE WORD "THAT" IN IT WHEN "THAT" FUNCTIONS CONJUNCTIVELY TO INTRODUCE A DEPENDENT CLAUSE.

Example:

I have often thought that the search for truth is never-ending.

You may be tempted to break this into two statements, "I have often thought" and "the search for truth is never-ending," but here the word "that" tells you that the latter part of the sentence completes the former part. Thus, there is only one statement being made here, so the sentence must be taken as a whole.

10) WORDS SUCH AS "IN ADDITION," "MOREOVER," AND "FURTHERMORE" ARE OFTEN INDICATIVE OF AN ADDITIONAL, INDEPENDENT ARGUMENT.

Example (Abelard writing about his castration):

[1]God's mercy had been kinder to me than to him (i.e., Origin), (for) [2]it was judged that he had acted most rashly and had exposed himself to no slight censure, whereas [3]the thing had been done to me through the crime of another, thus preparing me for a task similar to his own. {Moreover}, [4]it had been accomplished with much less pain, being so quick and sudden, (for) [5]I was heavy with sleep when they laid hands on me, and [6]felt scarcely any pain at all. (Peter Abelard, *The Secret of My Misfortune*)

Here "moreover" functions to pick out a second, independent line of argument for the conclusion.

Diagrammed:

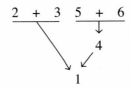

Section Four

ARGUMENT EVALUATION

Module Eight

A Closer Look at Statements

Preliminary to the evaluation of arguments, it is essential to be in a position to know precisely the meaning of the various statements that are its parts. The slightest "garnishment" (for instance, adding the word "perhaps" to a statement) can change the meaning of a statement in an argument radically and have a significant impact on one's evaluation of that argument. To this end, this module takes a closer look at statements.

1) THREE KINDS OF STATEMENTS

A) Necessary Truth

A necessary truth *statement that is true regardless of the way the world is at any given time.*

Example:

> Fabrice either went for a hike in the forest last Wednesday or she failed to do so on that day.

Strictly speaking, this statement is neither asserting that Fabrice took a hike on a particular day, nor is it asserting that she didn't. It merely asserts one *or* the other of two exclusive and exhaustive (i.e., contradictory) states of affairs. As such, it must be true. Moreover, because it asserts that one of two contradictory statements is true, without saying which of the two obtains, it is wholly uninformative. It follows that a necessary truth lacks empirical content, since its truth does not depend upon the way the world is at any point in time. To put it another way, this statement would be true in any possible world (for instance, a world in which gravity is an inverse-cubed repulsive force—instead of an inverse-square attractive force—or a world where life is possible in conditions of heat in excess of 1000 degrees C). Such statements are also called *tautologies*.

B) Necessary Falsehood

A necessary falsehood *is a statement that is false regardless of the way the world is at any given time.*

Example:

> Marco climbed up the tree at 3:00 last Sunday and he did not climb the tree at 3:00 last Sunday.

This statement, in contrast to a necessary truth, is very informative—in fact, overly so. In essence, it is so informative that it asserts both that a certain state of affairs *and* its contradictory are true, which is impossible. Like a necessary truth, a necessary falsehood lacks empirical content. This statement would be false in any possible world. Such statements are also called *self-contradictions*.

C) Contingent Statement

A contingent statement *is one whose truth is determined by the state of the world at a given time.*

Example:

> Alexander gave Roxanne the red blender she had requested.

Only contingent statements have empirical content—that is, their truth depends entirely upon the way the world is at some time. Here to see whether this statement is true or not, we merely try to find out whether Alexander did or did not give Roxanne the red blender she had requested.

2) COMPARING STATEMENTS

A) Contradictory Statements

Two statements, α and β, are contradictory *if whenever α is true β is false and whenever α is false β is true.*

Example:

1) Creation science is the true view of the origin of humans.
2) Creation science is not the true view of the origin of humans.

These two propositions are clearly contradictory in that the second is the denial of the first. Thus, the truth-value of the first will always be opposite the other.

B) Inconsistent Statements

Two statements, α and β, are inconsistent *if both α and β cannot be true at the same time. (They can, however, both be false.)*

Example:

1) God created the first organisms on land.
2) The first organisms arose naturally out of the sea through a slow course of development.

These two propositions are inconsistent in that they both cannot be true, though they both can be false.

C) Consistent Statements

Two statements, α and β, are consistent *if both α and β can be true at the same time.*

Example:

1) The first organisms arose from the sea through a slow course of development.
2) God is the ultimate cause of all things.

These statements seem inconsistent, but they are not. It is possible for both to be true. A creator could have set up things such that the first organisms arose from the sea.

D) Equivalent Statements

Two statements, α and β, are equivalent *if both α and β describe the exact state of affairs—that is, whenever α is true, so too is β, and whenever β is true, so too is α.*

Example:

1) Zoltan is a professional athlete.
2) Zoltan makes his living playing sports.

Any conceivable world where statement one is true would be a world where statement two is true also. Conversely, any world where statement one is false would be a world where statement two is false also. The truth-value of each is always the same under all possible conditions because they mean precisely the same thing.

3) MODAL STATEMENTS

A) Statements Involving Possibility

Example:

It is possible that the theory of evolution is false.

In general, statements involving possibility say very little. In effect, they are statements that deny the impossibility of some event. The example above is really asserting: "*It is not impossible that* the theory of evolution is false." In other words, it asserts that there is no contradiction involved in asserting the truth of this statement; in all, a very minimal assertion. In serious writing, such statements are only interesting when someone makes a claim that goes against what is generally held to be true. For instance, imagine a world-renown evolutionary biologist asserting the possibility of the theory of evolution being false. Immediately, we would want to know why she thinks this is possible. Uttered by someone who is not an expert on evolution, this statement would be uninteresting.

B) Statements Involving Necessity

Example:

> *It is necessary that* the theory of evolution is false.

Unlike statements involving possibility, statements involving necessity are very risky and say much. Here one wants to know not just why evolution is false, but why, since the statement is not a tautology, it is *necessary* that it is false. I shall have more to say about the modality of necessity below.

C) Statements Involving neither Possibility nor Necessity

Example:

> The theory of evolution is false.

On the one hand, this statement doesn't assert evolution *must be* false, so it says much less than a statement involving necessity. On the other hand, it is much more informative than a statement involving possibility.

4) ASSESSING ARGUMENTS
WITH MODAL CONCLUSIONS

A) Statements Involving neither Possibility nor Necessity

Example:

> Pablito likes most spicy foods.
> Burritos are spicy foods.
> So, Pablito will like burritos.

The conclusion involves neither possibility nor necessity, still it is a fairly bold statement. Yet it is given a reasonable amount of support by the premises.

B) Statements Involving Possibility/Probability

Example$_1$:

> Pablito likes most spicy foods.
> Burritos are spicy foods.
> So, Pablito will *probably* like burritos.

The conclusion, being a statement about probability, is weaker than "Pablito will like burritos." Since it is a weaker statement, the evidence of the premises makes the overall argument much stronger. (Consider also the conclusion "*It is possible that* Pablito will like burritos." This statement is so weak that the argument itself, though strong, is almost uninteresting.)

Example$_2$:

> Studies show that consumption of moderate amounts of alcohol is
>   strongly linked with prevention of heart disease.
> So, consumption of moderate amounts of alcohol *can* be beneficial for
>   health.

The view that consumption of alcohol in any amount is harmful has become so entrenched in modern thinking that studies that show moderate amounts having healthful consequences seem startling. The conclusion here is very informative.

In the main, statements involving possibility are very weak and uninteresting, except (1) when one view is so entrenched that any alternative seems impossible or (2) when pilot studies are done in science in an effort to establish the possibility of a link between two variables, such as consumption of alcohol and improved health.

C) Statements Involving Necessity

Example$_1$:

> Pablito likes most spicy foods.
> Burritos are spicy foods.
> So, *it is necessary that* Pablito will like burritos.

This conclusion is a statement involving necessity and, thus, a very bold statement. Very bold statements require much evidence in support of them. The modality of necessity here makes for a weak argument.

Example₂:

> Pablito likes *all* spicy foods.
> Burritos are spicy foods.
> So, *it is necessary that* Pablito will like burritos.

By making the first premise universal, the argument becomes deductive in that the premises now perfectly support the conclusion. In short, the truth of the premises necessarily makes the conclusion true, since the information in the conclusion is completely contained in the premises. So, prefacing the conclusion with "it is necessary that" is redundant and unneeded.

Note: People often use the modality of necessity in a rhetorically devious manner. Consider the following argument.

Example₃:

> Plutarch was an historian who was concerned more with writing about
>   people's virtue than writing about their history.
> So, *it must be the case that* Plutarch himself was a virtuous person.

Here the premise does not support the conclusion at all. As in the case above, often people preface conclusions in this way in an effort to force you to accept a statement that is poorly supported by evidence. Be cautious of the modality of necessity. Most of the time it is used, it is used wrongly.

D) Principle of Modality

The *principle of modality* (below) is a useful tool in assessing the strength of arguments where the conclusion contains a modal statement.

Adding the modality of possibility *to a conclusion of an argument will generally make the argument stronger; adding the* modality of necessity *to a conclusion will generally make it weaker.*

Note: In the main, be suspicious of modal words or phrases in arguments. Statements involving necessity are tremendously risky and are mostly out of place in all arguing, except formal philosophical works. Statements involving possibility are very weak and, for the most part, are only significant when such statements are considered to be impossible.

Module Nine

Conditions of Acceptance and Rejection

1) THE FUNCTION OF ARGUMENTS REVISITED

A) When to Accept an Argument

In module four, I mention that there are two conditions (the *conditions of acceptance*) that must be met before one is in a position to accept the conclusion of an argument as true. The first condition requires that each of the premises of an argument is true; the second condition requires that the premises, when assumed true, provide the right sort of support. To assure that these two conditions are met, ask yourself the following questions when analyzing an argument.

Are all the premises true?
Do the premises provide right type of support for conclusion?

Of course, it takes no special skills to answer the first question other than sober observation and a clear head. The difficulties come with the second question that concerns appropriateness. Thus, we shall be concerned almost exclusively with this second question.

To illustrate, I give four examples of arguments below (each decked out in standard form).

Argument$_1$:

1) All philosophers are lovers of wisdom.
2) Aristotle is a philosopher.
3) So, Aristotle is a lover of wisdom.

Clearly, in this example, the first condition is met. Both of the premises are true. Yet, even if they were not, the premises would provide the right kind of support (here absolute support) for the conclusion. So, both requirements are met and here, given that the support the premises give the conclusion is absolute, we would be foolish not to accept the conclusion as true.

Argument$_2$:

1) All women are animal-rights activists.
2) All animal-rights activists are maudlin people.
3) So, all women are maudlin people.

Here, of course, one should be suspicious because the conclusion is obviously false. Yet CA$_2$ is met: The premises provide complete support for the conclusion. The problem is that both premises are patently false. Recall that only one premise needs to be false for us to be in position to reject the conclusion.

Argument$_3$:

1) All humans are happy scavengers.
2) All androids are happy scavengers.
3) So, all humans are androids.

The problem with this argument should be obvious. Even if the premises were true, the conclusion wouldn't follow. There is something about the manner in which this argument is framed that makes us suspicious. Consider the same argument with different categories (that is, different subject and predicate terms).

Argument$_4$:

1) All giraffes are animals.
2) All wolverines are animals.
3) So, all giraffes are wolverines.

Here each of the premises is true, but the conclusion is still false. This is because the premises, when taken together, are not compelling evidence for the conclusion. One could readily accept both as true (and here one must), yet be justified in not accepting the conclusion. When CA_2 is met, the truth of the premises warrants acceptance of the conclusion as true.

B) When to Reject an Argument

In the previous section, we have answered the question of when to accept the conclusion of an argument as true by elaborating on two conditions that must be met. These we called the *conditions of acceptance*. To answer the question of when *not* accept the conclusion of an argument as true, I turn to the *condition of rejection.*

When either of the conditions of acceptance are not met, one is justified in not accepting a conclusion as true.

In short, one of two violations will occur:

CR_1: The argument will have at least one false premise.
CR_2: The premises will provide little or no support for conclusion, in which case, we shall have a fallacy.

In the case of CR_1, there is no reason to accept the truth of the conclusion (though it may be true). In the case of CR_2, there is no reason to accept the truth of the conclusion (though again it may be true).

2) THREE WAYS PREMISES CAN SUPPORT A CONCLUSION

A) The Premises, If True, Provide Incontrovertible Support for the Conclusion

Example:

1) All the cookies in the bin are oatmeal.
2) Filbert took a cookie from the bin.
3) So, Filbert took an oatmeal cookie.

In this example, the premises so completely support the conclusion that if they are true, the conclusion has to be true as well. This is called a *deductively valid argument*. Deductive validity is an all-or-nothing affair: The premises either fully support the conclusion or they fail to do so.

B) The Premises, If True, Provide a Reasonable Degree of Support for the Conclusion

Example:

1) Most cookies in the bin are oatmeal.
2) Filbert took a cookie from the bin.
3) So, Filbert took an oatmeal cookie.

In this example, if the premises are true, they make probable the truth of the conclusion. This is called an *inductively strong argument*. In contrast to deductive validity, inductive strength is a matter of degrees. The premises give us more reason to accept, rather than reject, the conclusion.

C) The Premises, If True, Provide *Little or No* Support for the Conclusion

Example$_1$:

1) Few of the cookies in the bin are oatmeal.
2) Filbert took a cookie from the bin.
3) So, Filbert took an oatmeal cookie.

This is an example of an inductive argument that is not strong—that is, its premises do not give us more reason to accept, rather than reject, the conclusion. Here the premises give little support for the conclusion. The conclusion may in fact be true, but we would not be rationally justified in believing it so on the basis of the premises.

Example$_2$:

1) All of the cookies in the bin are oatmeal.
2) Filbert took an oatmeal cookie.
3) So, Filbert took a cookie from the bin.

This is an example of a deductive argument that is not valid. It seems clear that the author of this argument intends that the conclusion follow necessarily from the premises. However, even if we grant the truth of the premises, the conclusion does not necessarily follow. Though the conclusion may in fact be true, we would not be rationally justified in believing it so because the premises do not provide incontrovertible support for the conclusion.

Module Ten

Three Common
Deductive Arguments

In this module, we look at three types of deductive arguments and one
fallacious form of each type. Remember that for deductive arguments
the support given by the premises is absolute (module nine). The right
sort of deductive argument, one that it valid, has premises that, if true,
give one no alternative other than to accept the conclusion as true.

1) MODUS PONENS (AFFIRMING THE ANTECEDENT)

Modus ponens, *meaning the affirming way, is a valid deductive argument with three statements: a conditional premise, a premise that affirms the antecedent of the conditional premise, and a conclusion that
affirms the consequent of the conditional premise.*

It has the following form:

1) If α, then β.
2) α.
3) So, β.

Example[1]:

> [1]Now you say that I believe in spiritual things. . . . But [2]if I believe in spir-
> itual things I must quite inevitably believe in spirits. (Plato, *Apology*)

In this argument, the conclusion is left unexpressed, but is implicitly understood as the consequent of statement two, "I must believe in spirits."

Standard form:

   1) Socrates believes in spiritual things
   2) If Socrates believes in spiritual things, then he must believe in spirits.
   3) [So, Socrates believes in spirits] (1 & 2).

Diagrammed:

$$\frac{1 + 2}{\downarrow}$$
$$3$$

Example$_2$:

   ¹You (Xeniades) must obey me (Diogenes the Cynic), although ²I am your slave; for, ³if a physician or a steersman were in slavery, he would be obeyed. (Diogenes Laertius, *Lives* VI.2)

The third statement is counterfactual. Its form implies that its antecedent is in fact false but that, if it were true, it would be sufficient to generate the truth of the conclusion.

Standard form:

   3) If a physician or a steersman were in slavery, he would be obeyed.
   2) Diogenes is a slave [and is like a physician or steersman].
   1) So, Diogenes should be obeyed.

Diagrammed:

$$\frac{3 + 2}{\downarrow}$$
$$1$$

Invalid form:

   1) If α, then β.
   2) β.
   3) So, α.

Here premise one tells us that the truth of α is sufficient to generate the truth of β. Premise two tells that that β is true. But since β is not sufficient to generate α, we can't be sure that α is true, given the truth of both premises. This deductive argument is formally distinct from modus ponens and invalid, since the premises poorly support the conclusion.

2) MODUS TOLLENS (DENYING THE CONSEQUENT)

Modus tollens, *meaning the denying way, is a valid deductive argument with three statements: a conditional premise, a premise that denies the consequent of the conditional premise, and a conclusion that affirms the denial of the antecedent of the conditional premise.*

It has the following form:

1) If α, then β.
2) Not β.
3) So, not α.

Example:

Let it be said at once then, that [1]if the bodies of the stars moved in a quantity either of air or of fire diffused throughout the whole, as everyone assumes them to do, the noise which they created would inevitably be tremendous, and this being so, it would reach and shatter things here on earth. Since, then, [2]this obviously does not happen, [3]their motions cannot in any instance be due either to soul or to external violence. (Aristotle, *On the Heavens*)

Diagrammed:

$$\frac{1 + 2}{3}$$

Invalid form:

1) If α, then β.
2) Not α.
3) So, not β.

Again premise one tells us that the truth of α is sufficient to generate the truth of β. Premise two tells that that α is not true. But since the denial of α is not sufficient to generate the denial of β, we can't be sure that not-β is true. This argument is formally distinct from modens tollens and invalid, as its premises poorly support the conclusion.

3) DISJUNCTIVE SYLLOGISM

Disjunctive syllogism *is a valid deductive argument with three statements: a disjunctive premise, a premise that denies all but one of the disjunctive statements, and a conclusion that affirms the one remaining disjunctive statement that has not been denied.*

It has the following form:

1) α, β, or γ.
2) Not α and not β.
3) So, γ.

Note: Here there are no limits to the number of disjunctive statements in the first statement: There can be two or twenty-two. It is only necessary that the second statement deny all but one of them for the argument to go through. I give two examples from Aristotle for illustration.

Example₁:

> [1]The states of the soul by which we always grasp the truth and never make mistakes, about what can or cannot be otherwise, are scientific knowledge, practical wisdom, wisdom, and intuition. But [2]none of the first three—practical wisdom, scientific knowledge, wisdom—is possible about origins. [3]The remaining possibility, then, is that we have intuition about origins. (Aristotle, *Nicomachean Ethics*)

Diagrammed:

$$\frac{1 + 2}{\downarrow}$$
$$3$$

Example₂:

> ~~Next we must examine what virtue is.~~ (Since) ¹there are three conditions arising in the soul—feelings, capacities and states—²virtue must be one of these. . . . First, then, ³neither virtues nor vices are feelings. . . . ⁴[T]he virtues are not capacities either. . . . ⁵If, then, the virtues are neither feelings nor capacities, the remaining possibility is that they are states."
> (Aristotle, *Nicomachean Ethics*)

The first proposition is irrelevant, so do not give it a number. Statement one generates statement two, which gets the disjunctive syllogism rolling. We can rewrite statement two as "Virtue must be a feeling, capacity, or state." Statement five is obviously the conclusion here, but it's not quite what we want, since it's in conditionalized form. However, we can rewrite it as the statement "The virtues are states," given the eliminative work of statement three. Let us put this in *standard form*, then diagram.

Standard form:

1) There are three conditions arising in the soul—feelings, capacities, and states.
2) So, virtues must be feelings, capacities, or states (1).
3) Neither virtues nor vices are feelings.
4) The virtues are not capacities either.
5) [So, the virtues are states] (3, 4, & 5).

Diagrammed:

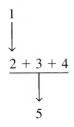

$$1$$
$$\downarrow$$
$$\underline{2 + 3 + 4}$$
$$\downarrow$$
$$5$$

Invalid form:

1) α or β.
2) α.
3) Not β.

The first premise asserts that α or β is true, or both. The second premise asserts that α is true. The truth of α, however, gives us no certainty that β is false, since the truth of both statements is consistent with the denial of the truth of the conclusion, not (not β), which is equivalent to β. Therefore, since the truth of the premises doesn't guarantee the truth of the conclusion, the argument is invalid.

Module Eleven

Common Inductive Arguments

In this module, we look at several types of inductive arguments. Remember that for inductive arguments the support given by the premises is a matter of degrees (module nine). The right sort of inductive argument, one that is strong, has premises that, if true, give one more reason than not to think that the conclusion too will be true. Strength varies, then, in proportion to the evidence given on behalf of a conclusion.

1) REDUCTIO AD ABSURDUM

Reductio ad absurdum *is an argument that begins with some initial supposition (some statement that is assumed true) and attempts to contradict that assumption (or show that it is absurd to believe it is true) by adding additional premises that are inconsistent with it or problematic.*

When a reductio argument is successful, there is good reason to believe that the initial supposition is false.

Example:

1) Miss Baramibee killed Mayor Boa (assumed true for sake of argument).
2) The mayor was seen by five different people at 8:00 p.m. on the night of the murder in his study and the body was found at 8:15 in his study.
3) So, the murder was committed between 8:00 and 8:15 p.m. (presumably in his study) (1).

4) Eight different people testify to having seen Miss Baramibee twenty miles away from the murder between the hours of 8:00 and 8:15 p.m.
5) So, if Miss Baramibee committed the murder, she must have been at the mayor's house between 8:00 and 8:15 and twenty miles away from the mayor's house at the same time (1 & 4).
6) So, Miss Baramibee could not have killed the mayor (5).

2) ANALOGICAL ARGUMENT

An analogical argument *is an argument that draws a conclusion about one thing (whether a particular thing or a class) based on the similarities it has with another thing.*

The overall strength of such arguments is, more often than not, difficult to assess, but much rides on the relevance of what is predicated of the things being compared. (Because of the difficulties involved in critically assessing such arguments, I maintain that you should use analogical arguments in your own philosophical writings only when more straightforward reasoning is impossible.)

Commonly seen form:

P has attributes α, β, and γ.
Q has attributes α, β, and γ.
P has attribute δ.
So, Q has attribute δ.

Of course, the number of things predicated in any of the statements can vary.

Standards of strength:

The things predicated of the subject terms (P and Q) in the first two premises (α, β, and γ) must be relevant to the thing or things predicated in the third premise and conclusion (δ). P and Q having α, β, and γ and P having δ must be good reasons to convince anyone that Q too must have δ.

There must be a lack of striking dissimilarities between P and Q. For instance, P may have attributes ε, ζ, η, *and* θ *that Q does not have, and these could be relevant and good reasons for Q not having* δ.

Example₁:

> Just as a sailor is one of a number of members of a community, so, we say, is a citizen. And though sailors differ in their capacities (for one is an oarsman, another a captain, another a lookout, and others have other sorts of titles) it is clear both that the most exact account of the virtue of each sort of sailor will be peculiar to him, and similarly that there will also be some common account that fits them all. For the safety of the voyage is a task of all of them, since this is what each of the sailors strives for. In the same way, then, the citizens too, even thought they are dissimilar, have the safety of the community as their task. (Aristotle, *Politics* III.4)

Standard form:

1) A sailor is a member of a ship.
2) A citizen is a member of a community.
3) There is a different account of virtue (i.e., different function) for each sort of sailor.
4) There is a different account of virtue (i.e., different function) for each sort of citizen.
5) Yet there is some common account of virtue for each sailor (i.e., the security of the ship).
6) So, likewise, there must be some common account of virtue for each citizen (i.e., the security of the city) (1–5).

Premises one and two are obvious enough. Assessment of the strength of this argument hinges on a critical evaluation of premises three through five.

Example₂:

> Magnanimous son of Tydeus, why ask of my lineage? Even as are the generations of leaves, so are those of men. As for the leaves, the wind blows them to the ground, but the forest, blooming, sends forth others, when it is the season of spring. Even so one generation of men spring up while another passes away. (Homer, *Iliad* VI)

Standard form:

1) The generations of leaves are like the generations of men.
2) The wind blows the leaves to the ground, but the blooming forest sends forth others in the season of spring.
3) So, one generation of men spring up while another passes away (1 & 2).

Here the first premises is a statement of comparison with nothing specific being compared (i.e., there are no attributes given). Still premises one and two do seem to give sufficient grounds for thinking the conclusion more likely to be true than false. The example can be formally presented as follows in a different manner:

P is similar to Q.
P has attribute α.
So, Q has attribute α.

Note: Premise one is unhelpfully vague. It tells us that P is similar to Q, but it does not tell us how it is similar to Q. Premise one tells us next to nothing about the two, since any two objects, however different, will always have *some* things in common. Be very cautious when assessing analogical arguments.

Overall, I believe that analogies in philosophy are misleading: They generally do more to muddle than clarify what one is attempting to say.

3) STATISTICAL SYLLOGISM

A statistical syllogism *is an argument that has two premises—one of which is a statistical statement that concerns a subject (i.e., "X% of Ps," "Few Ps," or "Most Ps") of which something is predicated (i.e., α) and the other of which is a particular statement—and a particular conclusion.*

General form:

X % of all Ps have α.
W is a P.
So, *W* has α.

Example$_1$:

1) 82% of kitchens are rooms redolent of onion.
2) This room is my kitchen.
3) So, this room is a room redolent of onion (1 & 2).

In assessing statistical syllogisms, roughly anything over 50% in premise one will make a strong argument. At least, anything over 50% will afford us more reason to think that the conclusion is true rather than false.

Standards of strength:

Strength is ascertained by premise one's proximity to 100% (i.e., the closer to 100%, the stronger the argument) or 0% (when the conclusion is negative; see below).
One must use all the available evidence in constructing or assessing such an argument.

Example$_2$:

1) 12% of the prospective job applicants are college educated.
2) Oblomov is a prospective job applicant.
3) So, Oblomov is *not* college educated (1 & 2).

Notice here that the first premise is a weak statement, but the argument is strong because the conclusion is the denial of the statement, "Oblomov is college educated." In asserting that 12% of the job applicants are college educated, premise one is also stating "88% of the prospective job applicants are *not* college educated." So, condition one is met.

When condition two is not met, we have the *fallacy of incomplete evidence*.

The fallacy of incomplete evidence *occurs when all of the available evidence is not used in an inductive argument.*

Example:

1) 98% of the attendants at a lush Hollywood bash are teetotalers.
2) W. C. Fields is an attendant.
3) So, W. C. Fields is a teetotaler (1 & 2).

It is generally known that W. C. Fields was very fond of imbibing alcohol. The argument, as given, commits the *fallacy of incomplete evidence*. It can be revised as follows and made strong:

Revised argument:

    1) 98% of the attendants at lush Hollywood bash are teetotalers.
    2) W. C. Fields is an attendant.
    3) W. C. Fields is a noted imbiber of strong spirits.
    4) So, W. C. Fields is *not* a teetotaler (1–3).

Note: As is characteristic of all inductive arguments, additional information (i.e., "W. C. Fields is a noted imbiber of strong spirits") to an argument that strongly supports "W. C. Fields is a teetotaler" winds up strongly supporting the contradictory statement, "W. C. Fields is *not* a teetotaler."

4) TYPES OF STATISTICAL SYLLOGISM

A) Argument from Authority

General form:

    Most of what authority *A* says about some topic P is true.
    A says α about P.
    So, α is true.

Strictly speaking, premise one should be assumed true only when the following conditions are met.

Standards of strength:

The authority must be expert in the area about which he speaks.
There must be general agreement among experts in that area.
The authority must be in agreement with the majority of other experts.

When each of these conditions is met, we have good reason to accept the first premise as true. Otherwise, we have the *fallacious argument from authority*.

The fallacious argument from authority *occurs when any of the three conditions listed above is not met.*

Note: Be on your guard for arguments that look like compelling appeals to authority that are poorly constructed.

Example:

1) Physicians are experts on medicines.
2) Most physicians give Zoon Aspirin to their patients more than any other brand.
3) So, Zoon Aspirin is better than all other brands.

In the main, aspirin is aspirin, and often the reason one brand is preferred by physicians over others is that they can get it at a discounted price. Here the conclusion does not follow, because premise two does not say that most physicians assert that Zoon Aspirin is *better* than all other brands, only that most give it to their patients.

B) Argument against the Man

General form:

Most of what someone S says about some topic P is false.
S says α about P.
So, α is false.

This argument, of course, will be strong or weak, depending upon the truth of the first premise. In general, we shall seldom be in a position to assume its truth, for there is a general inclination in people not to talk about things concerning which they are ignorant. So be chary and suspicious when you come across such an argument. It is probable that premise one will be justified by nothing other than personal dislike.

C) Argument from Consensus

General form:

Most of what the majority of people say about any topic P is true.
The majority of people say α.
So, α is true.

Example:

1) Most Americans believe that angels exist.
2) So, angels exist.

The problem with this argument type is obvious. As Plato constantly reminded his audience, the majority is seldom, if ever, in a position to be experts on any issue. Arguments of this type, however, are useful when consensus, not truth, is at stake. We might, for example, want to decide whether or not taxes should be raised and so we appeal to a consensus of opinion.

5) INDUCTIVE GENERALIZATION

An inductive generalization *is a type of inductive argument that goes from particular premises to a generalized conclusion.*

Note: This is often mistakenly assumed to be a definition that applies to all inductive arguments (a mistake made by many dictionaries today).

Example$_1$:

Chimp$_1$ is capable of mastering certain linguistic signs.
Chimp$_2$ is capable of mastering certain linguistic signs.
Chimp$_n$ is capable of mastering certain linguistic signs.
So, all chimps are capable of mastering certain linguistic signs.

Revised argument:

Some number "n" of *observed* chimps are capable of mastering certain linguistic signs.
So, *all* chimps are capable of mastering certain linguistic signs.

Example$_2$:

50% of the time I've taken a philosophy class I've gotten a 'D'.
So, *50% of all* the philosophy classes I'll ever take I'll get a 'D'.

The first example has a universal generalization as a conclusion, while the second has a statistical generalization as one.

General form:

> X% of *observed* Ps have α.
> So, X% of *all* Ps have α (where X may be 100%).

How will you know when to accept the conclusion of such an argument as true? For instance, both of the examples above do not seem strong. Why not?

Standards of strength:

The sample in the premise must be sufficiently varied.
The sample in the premise must be sufficiently large.

To ensure variety, a *random sample* should be taken from a population. This guarantees, insofar as this is possible, that each member of a population has an equal chance of being selected. Concerning size, in the main, if the sample is taken from a population with finite size, the larger the sample, the surer we can be that this sample closely resembles the population.

6) FALLACIES RELATED TO INDUCTIVE GENERALIZATIONS

A) Hasty Generalization

A hasty generalization *is an inductive generalization whose sample size is too small to secure the truth of the conclusion.*

Example:

1) Madame Luna predicted in 1980 the fall of Russian communism.
2) So, Madame Luna is a reputable psychic.

To see why this argument is not strong, we need only to revise it as follows.

Revised argument:

1) One observed prediction of Madame Luna has come true.
2) So, all of Madame Luna's predictions must be true.

Here the assessment of Luna's psychic capacities actually rests on a judgment based on one instance. It fails also to take into consideration any failed predictions or any other successes.

B) Biased Sample

Biased sample *is an inductive generalization whose sample lacks sufficient variation to guarantee the truth of the conclusion.*

Example:

1) 70% of the 200 people that I interviewed at the new food gallery in the library thought that the money to build it was well spent.
2) So, 70% of all people think that the money for the library's new food gallery was money well spent.

Here, of course, the difficulty occurs because the interviewing occurred *only* at the food gallery. One would fully expect that people eating there would likely approve of it.

Module Twelve

Other Common Fallacies

In module ten, three common types of deductive arguments are listed—modus ponens, modus tollens, and disjunctive syllogism—along with a corresponding fallacious form for each type. In the previous module, some of the most common inductive arguments as well as certain related inductive fallacies are given.

In this module, we begin with a more generic definition of fallacy than the one given in module four, and then some of the most frequently encountered fallacies are given. While reading, try to explain why each of the examples listed below is an instance of the type of fallacy described or defined. (Some of these fallacies have been alluded to or listed earlier.)

1) WHAT IS A FALLACY?

A fallacy *is a mistake in reasoning which occurs for reasons other than false premises.*

2) FALLACIES OF RELEVANCE

A) Accident

The fallacious argument from accident *occurs when one applies a general rule to a particular instance that it was not meant to cover.*

Example:

> Excessive noise in public places is generally frowned upon, so you should not cheer at the hockey game when the Detroit Red Wings score a goal.

B) Appeal to Force

The argument from force *is fallacious reasoning that appeals to force, not evidence, as a means of persuasion.*

Example:

> The CEO Milovich's policies must be correct, for all who have disagreed with them have lost their jobs.

C) Appeal to Pity

The argument from pity *is a fallacious appeal to pity in order to have some statement accepted as true.*

Example:

> You've got to give me at least a "B" in Logic, because I'll lose my scholarship if you don't and I can't continue on with my education without my scholarship.

D) Missing the Point

The fallacy of missing the point *occurs when the evidence in the premises leads plainly to a conclusion other than the one that is given.*

Example:

> Down's syndrome children cannot experience many of the joys of life that other children can, so we ought to abort any such fetus.

E) Red Herring

The fallacy of red herring *happens when you ignore an attack on an argument you have given by diverting your critic's attention to another issue.*

Example:

> Gunderpugg believes in women's rights, but he doesn't want to see a
> women's professional football league. Therefore, Gunderpugg doesn't re-
> ally believe in gender equity.

F) Straw Man

The straw-man fallacy *occurs when you present an opponent's argument in a weak form so that it can be easily refuted.*

Example:

> Freudian psychoanalysis is patently absurd. No one can trust a scientist
> who gets inspiration from mythology.

Here the issue is not where Freud drew his inspiration (i.e., the myth of
Oedipus), but whether or not his theory of psychoanalysis, based on the
Oedipus Complex, is correct. Scientists draw inspiration from the
strangest sources.

3) STATISTICAL FALLACIES AND OTHER FALLACIES OF WEAK INDUCTION

A) Appeal to Ignorance

The argument from appeal to ignorance *occurs when you argue falla-
ciously that something is true (or false) because no one has proven it
false (or true).*

Example:

> No one has shown that there is not intelligent life on other planets, so life
> must exist on another planet somewhere.

The problem here is that lack of evidence for some statement, say p, is
itself not evidence for its denial, not p. Lack of evidence is just this —
lack of evidence — and it cannot be used as evidence for a contradictory
statement.

B) Biased Sample

The fallacious argument from biased sample *happens when you try to support a general statement with an unvaried sample (see also module eleven).*

Example:

> 78% of all the students interviewed at Colby College endorsed the democratic candidate, so 78% of all people in Maine endorse the democratic candidate.

C) Hasty Generalization

The fallacy of hasty generalization *occurs when there is an inadequate amount of evidence to ground a general statement (see also module eleven).*

Example:

> Each of the three classes I've taken at the University of Michigan was difficult. It must be the case that all their classes are difficult.

D) Slippery Slope

The slippery-slope fallacy *comprises a conclusion that rests upon a supposed chain reaction suggested by the premises when there is no reason to believe that such a reaction will take place.*

Example:

> Belgian beers are being imported to America at a rate that is 500% greater than that of 10 years ago. It follows that in 10 more years, everyone in America will be drinking Belgian beers.

4) CAUSAL FALLACIES

A) Gambler's Fallacy

The gambler's fallacy *happens when you assume that two independent events (i.e., events that have no impact on each other) are actually dependent.*

Example:

> Aristides won money each of the last three times he's played the slots at
> Greektown Casino, so he'll win money when he plays slots tomorrow.

Slots, at casinos, are mathematically arranged so as, on average, to give
players some percentage of what they put into the machine on each
play.

B) Genetic Fallacy

The genetic fallacy *happens when you confuse the origin of some statement with evidence for it.*

Example:

> God exists because I was told so when I was young.

Here being told that God exists when young explains how one has come
to believe that God exists, but it is not any sort of evidence on behalf of
the existence of God.

C) Ignoring a Common Cause

The fallacy of ignoring a common cause *amounts to attributing falsely
one of the effects of a cause as a cause for another of the effects of the
same (undisclosed) cause.*

Example:

> When the days get shorter and the nights get longer in Canada, the tem-
> perature drops. Consequently, the shortness of each day is the cause of the
> drop in temperature.

It is the path and inclination of the sun during winter that comes into
play here.

D) Post Hoc (ergo Propter Hoc)

The post-hoc fallacy *(literally, "after this, (therefore because of this)")* *occurs when you attribute causal force to some event simply because it occurred prior to some other event.*

Example:

> When Amiere helped a blind person to cross the street the other day, she found a fifty-dollar bill on the other side of the street. Who can doubt that kindness pays?

5) OTHER FALLACIES

A) Amphiboly

The fallacy of amphiboly *happens when you argue to a conclusion from one or more sentences that are syntactically ambiguous.*

Example:

> Rhonda related to Rhenny that that she had the necklace. So, Rhenny had the necklace.

B) Begging the Question

The fallacy of begging the question *occurs when you arrive at a conclusion from premises that are themselves suspicious and in need of justification.*

Example:

> Everything has some cause, so the universe too must have a cause.

C) Composition

The fallacy of composition *occurs when you argue that what is true of something's parts is also true of it as a whole.*

Example:

> Each member of the New York Yankees is good, so the New York Yan-
> kees are a good baseball team.

D) Division

The fallacy of division *occurs when you argue that what is true of something's whole must also be true of its parts.*

Example:

> The community of Birmingham is wealthy, so each of its citizens must be
> wealthy.

E) Equivocation

The fallacy of equivocation *is an argument where a word is used in one
sense in one part of an argument and in another sense in another part.*

Example:

> Chapter 21 is the end of the book. The end of everything is some good
> thing. Therefore, chapter 21 will be good.

F) False Dichotomy

The fallacy of false dichotomy *occurs when a conclusion is supported
by a disjunctive premise (an "or" statement) whose truth is suspect
(i.e., the disjunctive statement is not exclusive and exhaustive).*

Example:

> Either Garriston Fluffs eats spare ribs each day or he gets horribly de-
> pressed. Since Garriston doesn't want to be depressed, he must eat spare
> ribs daily.

Here it seems very likely that Garriston's not eating ribs is no direct
cause of depression, but perhaps a justification of a bad habit.

Section Five

GENERAL WRITING TIPS

Module Thirteen

Getting Ready to Write

1) FORMATTING AND STRUCTURING YOUR PAPER

These suggestions for formatting are merely helpful hints in order for you to have a certain degree of uniformity to all your papers.

Use one-inch margins all around your paper.

Use left alignment instead of justification.

Use double spacing throughout.

Inset the first line of each new paragraph ¼ or ½ inch. Do not use an extra space between paragraphs.

Inset lengthy quotes. This inset should be consistent with your formatting of the first line of each paragraph (i.e., ¼ or ½ inch). Keep these double-spaced.

Use a 12-point font that is clearly readable. Stay away from fancy fonts. Times New Roman is one that many publishers prefer.

If notes are necessary, use endnotes, not footnotes.

Give your paper a title.

Include references throughout and a bibliography section (see modules seventeen and eighteen).

2) GENERAL TIPS FOR WRITING

A) Be Structured!

Structure your essays by preparing, in advance, a thesis (module four) and an outline (modules seventeen and eighteen). Develop a very narrow thesis for short papers. Tackle a small issue. If the question given to you admits of a lengthy response, narrow your thesis with your teacher's permission to address only some part of the question. You may even want to explain to readers in your introductory section what it is you are *not* going to try to accomplish in your essay. Overall, never give readers the sense that there is much more to the issue that is left unsaid by the end of your paper. Let your thesis and outline guide you completely throughout.

B) Be Coherent!

Coherence of thought demonstrates just how well you understand the issues involved. Present your arguments *tightly*. Make sure that your paper flows throughout in a manner that makes the overall argument clear to a reader. Draw from the readings plentifully to support the points that you are making (without excessive use of direct quotes) and reference all such points.

C) Be Relevant!

Make sure that everything you write is directly relevant to the issue you are addressing. If you are given a question to answer, answer it *directly*. Never stray from the topic to shed light on some irrelevant issue in an effort to impress your teacher. Teachers are more impressed by your essay's focus, not by your knowledge on irrelevant issues. Remember, there will be other days to write on other issues.

D) Be Analytical!

Spend the lion's share of your time developing your thesis with arguments instead of summarizing the readings. Remember this is a *critical analysis* of the material. Break down the argument(s) you encounter and give an assessment of them. It is your own thinking that counts here.

E) Be Fluid!

Write simply and plainly, and avoid verbiage. Strive for fluidity, but not in a stream-of-consciousness manner. Your essays should read easily from sentence to sentence, from paragraph to paragraph. While striving for fluidity, keep in mind the significance of coherence and relevance.

F) Be Creative!

Present your view uniquely by trying to find some position on an issue that has not yet been defended. This, of course, requires that you first have a good grasp of what others have said on this issue. If you defend a thesis that is similar to someone else's thesis, show clearly how your view differs from (and is preferable to) this thesis. Again, along these lines, do not spend too much time reviewing in book-report fashion what it is you are going to evaluate.

G) Be Sympathetic!

Construct digestible paragraphs. Don't have paragraphs that are so long or dense that readers don't have a chance to catch their breath. Remember, the end of each paragraph gives readers a chance to pause and reflect on what was just said. If a paragraph is too lengthy or contains too much information, you can easily loose a reader. Keep paragraphs relatively short and digestible.

H) Be Honest!

Reference all points that need referencing. As a general rule of thumb, if you make any statement and that statement did not originate from you, but came from a reading, then this statement must be referenced (whether or not you quote directly!). *Failure to do so amounts to stealing ideas from another author—plagiarism.* Plagiarism is a very serious offense in academic circles.

I) Be Yourself!

For short papers, stay away from excessive quoting from other sources. This gives a short paper a cut-and-paste feel to it. It reads choppily and lacks fluidity. Only quote when (1) the author's wording defies restatement (it is so perfectly stated that to do other than quote it would be a disservice, but this is *very* rare) or (2) you are planning on attacking something this author has said (and there is something about the wording that is crucial to your attack).

J) Be Accurate!

If you are evaluating an argument, reconstruct the author's views faithfully and accurately *before* you begin critical analysis of that view. Sometimes perceived problems with another's view vanish when you take the time to reconstruct accurately the arguments on behalf of it. Here especially the analytic tips and rules for diagramming in modules five and seven come into play. Remember the straw-man fallacy!

K) Be Charitable!

If you are not quite sure what an author means by some statement and, for instance, it seems clear that there can be only two possible interpretations, *if* you must choose between these, then choose the most favorable of the two alternatives. In other words, choose the interpretation that makes best sense of this author's general line of argument. If an author's view is genuinely ambiguous (i.e., if there is more than one possible interpretation that is consistent with the main line of argument and there is no reason to favor one over another), point this out in your criticism. In general, however, stay away from criticizing works you do not fully understand.

L) Be Careful!

When you've finished your essay, proofread it carefully. If possible, have a colleague proof it for you. When proofing, subject the whole essay to critical analysis. Is your thesis clearly stated? Are the arguments on behalf of it plainly presented? Are there grammatical and spelling mistakes? Does your essay deviate from your outline? (See module nineteen for more on revising and rewriting your essay.)

M) Be Proud!

I give this as the last tip for, in a sense, I consider it to be the most important one. The reason is that if you can take pride in the process of creating a philosophical essay, then the other tips will be easy to follow. Remember, this is *your* paper and it has *your* name just beneath its title. As your work, it is an extension of you and, thus, it tells others much about the type of person you are. Treat it as you would a work of art.

Writing Your Thesis

The next three modules offer tips to improve your writing. This module is about writing a sound philosophical thesis. The next module concerns the main body of the paper—i.e., the arguments in support of your thesis. The sixteenth module details common writing mistakes. In these modules, there are several suggestions for improvement and many examples to illustrate these suggestions. These examples come from students' papers throughout my years of teaching philosophy.

1) GIVE YOUR THESIS A CONTEXT.

Example:

> What would you do? I agree with the view that Glaucon expresses and explains. Justice by his definition is about self-fulfillment without punishment.

This is thrown out at the start of a short essay and left on its own (presumable as a thesis). Give readers a context. This is a paper that concerns the story of the ring of Gyges from Book II of Plato's *Republic*.

Rewritten:

> In Book II of Plato's *Republic*, through his illustration of the ring of Gyges, Glaucon argues that justice is about self-fulfillment without punishment. In this paper, I argue that this view of justice is essentially correct.

2) AVOID WRITING A VAGUE OR AMBIGUOUS THESIS.

Example$_1$:

> The topic I chose to write about is heroes.

This tells us something about the general topic of the paper, but nothing about the direction of the paper. What is it about this thesis that would make anyone want to read on?

Example$_2$:

> In this essay, I argue with Feinberg (although he doesn't really take a firm stand either way) that pornography can be art.

If Feinberg doesn't take a clear stand either way on pornography being art, why would one agree with him? Moreover, it's quite unlikely that a professional philosopher would be capable of publishing an article without taking a stance on an issue.

Example$_3$:

> In this essay you will read about Socrates' argument with Meletus. This essay has my view of what I thought Socrates meant and it will also critically analyze his argument. I feel that Socrates has an argument that lacks some reasonable thought, and will discuss it in depth. But what if things didn't go the way they did? I will try to explain what might have happened if things were different.

Which argument is being referred to? What direction will the analysis take? How does it lack reasonable thought? What are the events referred to and how might they have gone otherwise? Nothing here hooks the reader. Every sentence is vague.

3) KEEP THE THESIS AND CLAIMS ABOUT THE DIRECTION OF YOUR PAPER SIMPLE.

Example:

> In his article "Is Homosexuality Bad Sexuality Because It Is Biologically Unnatural?" Michael Ruse addresses questions regarding the morality, or

immorality, of homosexuality. The aim of this paper is to summarize Ruse's claims regarding the morality of homosexuality, citing potential weaknesses that, if corrected, could strengthen the argument. In addition to the summary, a brief discussion regarding an important omission is included. A discussion regarding the perverseness of homosexuality is not included in this paper.

This paragraph does give the reader insight and direction into the paper, but it could be simplified.

Rewritten:

In his article "Is Homosexuality Bad Sexuality Because It Is Biologically Unnatural?" Michael Ruse addresses questions regarding the morality of homosexuality. The aim of this paper is to summarize Ruse's claims and cite potential weaknesses that, if corrected, could strengthen the argument. In addition, I include a brief discussion regarding an important omission.

Although rewritten, this still suffers from another problem, which leads us to the following suggestion.

4) MAKE YOUR THESIS SPECIFIC.

Example:

In the essay I am about to write, I would like to discuss the Epicurean view of friendship. Although many have criticized and labeled this view as inconsistent and contradictory, and that is what I would like to discuss.

This thesis, second sentence, doesn't say much at all. State *precisely* what it is you are going to discuss, but first, set up the problem with something illustrative of Epicurus' view of friendship.

Rewritten:

Among the fragments that survive, Epicurus gives a view of friendship that is seemingly contradictory. As an egoist hedonist, he is committed to the view that all things are valuable only insofar as they bring about pleasure, yet he states that friendship, like pleasure, is intrinsically valuable. In this paper, I aim to show that this tension can be resolved.

5) GO BEYOND DESCRIPTION IN YOUR THESIS; FOCUS ON A CRITICAL ANALYSIS.

Example₁:

> Mill states that individual freedom is in the best interest of humankind for the prosperity of society.

This is an obviously true statement to anyone familiar with Mill's work, *On Liberty*. Evaluative essays have a critical component. So, an evaluative thesis should have a critical component.

Rewritten:

> Mill states that individual freedom is in the best interest of humankind for the prosperity of society. In this essay, I shall argue, in agreement with Mill, that individual freedom is indeed a societal good, however, in doing so, I show that Mill's notion of prosperity is flawed.

Example₂:

> In John Stuart Mill's book, *On Liberty*, Mill's thesis is written on the opinion that Mill believes the way to deal with an individual who harms others while exercising his idea of liberty is that you must punish them, physically or morally, and teach them right from wrong.

This is a very wordy thesis statement that lacks a critical component.

Rewritten:

> In *On Liberty*, Mill argues that those who harm others must be punished or educated. In my paper, I argue that Mill's thesis is correct, but that his notion of punishment is too vague to be serviceable.

6) WRITE A THESIS THAT AIMS AT ENGAGING, NOT TURNING OFF, READERS.

Example$_1$:

> The Epicurus view between justice and friendship is indeed interesting. The views on justice and friendship are well worth comparing, although the interpretation of the Epicurean views on the two are curiously imaginative. In other words, Epicurus had an interesting view on the relationship between justice and friendship.

Not only is this thesis vague, it is also uninteresting. Does this make you as a reader want to read on? As I state in module fifteen, the word "interesting" should be avoided at all costs in essays. It's vague and can always be replaced by something more specific. What does it mean for the thesis to be "curiously imaginative" and why is this something undesirable?

Example$_2$:

> The question here is whether Aristotle's doctrine of the mean is a viable ethic for today. My answer and according to what little I understand about Aristotle's ethics is that it is a viable ethic.

Here we have an objection similar to that of the prior example. In telling readers that you have a poor grasp of the topic about which you're writing, you turn off readers from your topic. Imagine a sports analyst who begins a one-hour special on baseball by stating he doesn't know much about the game he'll be critiquing in the full hour. Who would watch?

7) TRY NOT TO DO TOO MUCH WITH YOUR THESIS.

Example:

> Is winning an obsession for athletes in sports? I will look at aspects of competition with regards to winning. I am also looking into whether the playoff system that has been established in professional sports in the United States actually determines the best team from that season.

Here, in effect, we have two theses: one about the obsession with winning in sports and another about whether or not the playoff system determines the best team. Two separate topics make for two papers. Don't force the two into one just because you have something to say about both issues. Choose the topic that most interests you and leave the other aside for another time.

Module Fifteen

General Writing Tips

The previous module dealt with tips for writing a good philosophical thesis. This module gives several tips for the body of your essay.

1) AVOID VAGUE OR AMBIGUOUS CLAIMS THROUGHOUT YOUR PAPER.

Example₁:

> Fromm was a psychologist who dealt with many different and equally difficult issues.

That Fromm wrote on many different issues is obvious and, so, uninteresting. That each of these was equally difficult is certainly false. The overall problem is the vagueness of "difficult." Remember, philosophy is a discipline that strives for clarity through elimination of such vague claims.

Example₂:

> I agree with MacIntyre for the most part, but he made a few points in which I believe to be false.

The phrase "for the most part" is horribly vague. Moreover, don't say that *some* of the things MacIntyre said are false, state what these claims are.

Example$_3$:

> It is believed by some scholars that by the year 2010, we will have doubled the world's knowledge, and every five years after that it will double again. Theoretically, by the year 2015, we should be almost four times as smart as we are now.

Doubling the amount of knowledge does not make each person four times as smart by 2015, and it will not make those born at 2015 and after four times as smart as those born before. In short, the phrase "four times as smart" makes little sense. It is best to say that the total amount of information available to anyone will have quadrupled by the year 2015.

2) NEVER BRING UP AN INTERESTING, ISOLATED POINT AND LEAVE IT UNEXPLAINED OR UNJUSTIFIED. ELABORATE OR OMIT IT!

Example$_1$:

> I feel it evident that Freud's argument of the origins of religion is, in fact, faulty. It seems that under the right circumstances, Freud could be right in his beliefs. . . .

Though this is given out of context, the first statement is never justified in the rest of the paper. The second claim, though vague, seems that it might be informative, if spelled out clearly. The biggest problem is that nothing further is said concerning it. Readers, then, are teased with the expectation that there will be something said about this claim later. There isn't, and so the writer leaves his readers with a sense of frustration.

Example$_2$:

> Diogenes was also referred to as "Socrates gone mad."

This is an extremely engaging claim, yet this writer says nothing more on this issue. Elaborate on it or omit it altogether.

3) NEVER BRING UP ONE TOPIC ONLY
TO SAY THAT YOU'LL GET BACK TO IT LATER.

Example:

> Sextus Empiricus lived in the second century a.d. Before we get into his life, the idea of Skepticism must be looked into.

Go into Skepticism first (in a paragraph or so), if this is your aim, then introduce Sextus thereafter.

4) AVOID STATING THE OBVIOUS.

Example$_1$:

> Based on the definition of genetic fallacy stated above, it seems that Freud does not commit the genetic fallacy when he traced the origin of religion. This can be seen when looking at his writing.

The last sentence is superfluous. Where else would one expect to find evidence of the genetic fallacy?

Example$_2$:

> Rawls begins where most great philosophers do, at the beginning.

What is wrong with this is too obvious to need spelling out.

Example$_3$:

> Along with the many similarities (between Gandhi and Aristotle) there are also many differences.

As I mention in the previous module, always steer clear from the similarity-difference type of claim.

5) AVOID MAKING INSIPID CLAIMS.

Example$_1$:

> Some perverted acts, like necrophilia, are clearly wrong and therefore immoral. It is not right to take advantage of a corpse.

A corpse is a dead, non-sentient human being. How can one take advantage of something non-sentient? This, of course, is a good sign that the author did not spend much time rereading and revising the essay.

Example$_2$:

> All reasons or examples set aside, I believe that homosexuality is not immoral.

Why would anyone, writing a paper on philosophy, something that is essentially critical, want to set aside reasons and examples?

6) NEVER TALK OF YOUR OWN MISUNDERSTANDING OF A PAPER OR BOOK IN YOUR ESSAY.

Example:

> I do not completely understand Garry's arguments for why pornography is degrading and immoral.

Why write about something you don't completely understand? Read it until you do understand it or write about something else.

7) AVOID EXAGGERATED CLAIMS.

Example:

> I disagree with just about everything Russell has ever written.

This would not be a problem, if this student had read everything Russell has written, but this is certainly not the case.

8) DON'T SHOOT DOWN YOURSELF OR ANYONE ELSE WHEN WRITING.

Example₁:

> Of course, this is just my opinion on this subject, and everything I've said has to be taken with a grain of salt.

This functions mostly to undermine your credibility as someone who is knowledgeable on the subject on which you are writing. Let your claims stand or fall because of the evidence supporting them.

Example₂:

> Plato's theory of forms is quite ridiculous. Aristotle was a much smarter philosopher.

Plato's theory is not at all ridiculous. State precisely what it is that you find objectionable about Plato's views and go from there. Hasty criticism of one of the world's greatest thinkers is very presumptuous.

9) WRITE SIMPLY.

Example₁:

> In this essay, I collaborate with John Stuart Mill that individuality benefits the whole of society. Of course, for any of this to partake, there must be individuality.

This author uses the words "collaborate" and "partake" wrongly. Steer clear from words that you do not completely grasp.

Example₂:

> Contemporary society is riddled with negative constituents that manifest themselves in the varied forms of violence, ignorance, racism, and apathy. It has been argued that these problems stem from an inadequate system of societal indoctrination in the school system, and this must hold at least some marginal degree of truth.

This is stodgy, stuffy, wordy, and unclear! You can get the same point across more simply.

Rewritten:

> Society today is riddled with violence, racism, ignorance, and apathy. Some have argued that these problems are in part the result of defects in our educational system. I agree.

10) KEEP YOUR OPINIONS, BELIEFS, FEELINGS, ETC. THAT CONCERN THE WRITING OF THE ESSAY OUT OF YOUR PAPER.

Example$_1$:

> I found Aristotle's *Nicomachean Ethics* to be difficult reading. . . .

This has absolutely nothing to do with the development of a thesis. Leave it completely out. Remember, formal papers are not journal entries.

Example$_2$:

> So how necessarily does one educate man so that he's wise in the area of conflict? Please excuse the use of the word "man" instead of "mankind." I'd rather address the human race as man as opposed to mankind. This by no means is a chauvinistic move on my part. It's merely a way for me to address the human race in a more personal way.

Here we have three sentences that take readers nowhere and have no part in a philosophical essay. This student goes off on a stream-of-consciousness tangent.

11) STAY AWAY FROM THE USE OF ITALICS.

Example:

> Alexander has a mind uncluttered by *trivial* concerns.

The sense of this sentence is clear enough without having to italicize "trivial." Doing so suggests readers will not get the sense of a claim without emphasis, which is unlikely. If you are intent upon using italics, do so sparingly.

12) STAY AWAY FROM WORDY EXPRESSIONS.

Examples:

Instead of . . .	*Choose . . .*
There is no doubt that . . .	Doubtless . . .
She is a woman who . . .	She . . .
His account is a false one.	His account is false.
This is a subject that . . .	This subject . . .
used for pedagogical purposes . . .	used for pedagogy . . .
the question as to . . .	whether . . .
call your attention to the fact that . . .	remind you . . .
owing to the fact that . . .	since . . .
The author attempts to enforce her point by . . .	She states . . .

There are, of course, numerous other instances of verbosity. As a rule, once you've finished a paper, go through it thoroughly and try to simplify wherever you can.

13) KEEP COORDINATE IDEAS IN THE SAME FORM.

Example:

The science of biology is fertile, while the mathematical science is sterile.

Rewritten:

The science of biology is fertile, while the science of math is sterile.

Here the rewritten form has clarity of exposition that the example lacks. It's even, I dare say, a bit more elegant.

14) STAY AWAY FROM METAPHORICAL EXPRESSIONS.

Three Examples:

> Even though his ignorance may be apparent, his intelligence stings like a sword as he cuts Gorgias with several blows.
> One topic that I do not think that a lot of people take a step back to evaluate is how individuality plays a part in progressive societies. Many times people just go with the flow of what is happening in their lives, and do not think twice if someone who is higher up on the ladder may have made the wrong decision.
> The series of speeches in *Symposium* are not simply meant as beating around the bush that leads us to the main event.

Metaphors may be fun to put into papers, but there is little, if any, use for them in papers on philosophy. Philosophy is about clarity and metaphors detract from clarity. The first example creates a vivid, but tremendously exaggerated scenario that is very misleading. Examples two and three are vague.

15) NEVER INTRODUCE A PASSAGE BY TALKING ABOUT ITS LOCATION IN A PARTICULAR PUBLICATION.

Example:

> In his paragraph beginning on page 127, MacIntyre says. . . .

Put this information either in a footnote or in parentheses at the end of the sentence (see module seventeen).

16) CHOOSE THE ACTIVE VOICE IN PREFERENCE TO THE PASSIVE VOICE.

Example:

> Plato's views were thoroughly criticized by Aristotle.

Rewritten:

Aristotle thoroughly criticized Plato's views.

In general, the active voice gives readers a sense of involvement that is lacking with the passive voice. It's also slightly less wordy.

17) WHEN YOU DO NOT UNDERSTAND SOMETHING AN AUTHOR HAS SAID, NEVER ASSUME THAT THE AUTHOR IS CONFUSED. IT IS VERY LIKELY THAT THE CONFUSION IS YOUR OWN.

Example:

Hume was confused by this issue. . . . He probably did not make this issue clear for the issue itself cannot be cleared up by Hume.

David Hume, for instance, was an exceptionally lucid thinker. A thorough reading and rereading of his work would likely clear up any confusion.

18) AVOID SWEEPING GENERALIZATIONS OR BOLD CLAIMS THAT CANNOT BE SUPPORTED BY SUFFICIENT EVIDENCE.

Example:

I strongly disagree with the article "Is Our Admiration of Sports Heroes Fascistoid?" written by Torbjörn Tännsjö.

One cannot "strongly disagree" with a whole article. This, I suppose, amounts to disagreeing with each and every claim. One can disagree with its thesis, many of its claims, or the general tenor of its line of argument. State precisely what it is that you find objectionable.

19) NEVER USE YOUR OWN PERSONAL EXPERIENCE AS EVIDENCE FOR A GENERALIZATION. PERSONAL EXPERIENCE CAN BE USED TO ILLUSTRATE A POINT, NOT TO JUSTIFY IT.

Example:

> From my own experience, I have found competition in sport does not have deleterious consequences, so I find it hard to believe it can be harmful to society.

This amounts to sloppy inductive reasoning (see "hasty generalization," module twelve). Look for empirical support for generalizations such as these. Use your own experience merely as confirmation or an illustration, instead of justification.

Common Mistakes

1) GRAMMATICAL MISTAKES

A) Misplaced Participial Phrases

Example$_1$:

> Beatrice told the truth to Alush, not being one to lie.

The participial phrase, "not being one to lie" modifies "Alush," since it follows it directly. It should follow directly after "Beatrice." Correctly stated: "Beatrice, not being one to lie, told the truth to Alush."

Example$_2$:

> Being the person best suited for the job, the president hired Roseanne immediately.

Placing the participial phrase just before "the president" implies that "the president" is being modified, not "Roseanne."

Rewritten:

> The president immediately hired Roseanne, being the best person for the job."

B) Problems with Pronouns

Example₁:

> Nevea and Phoenicia agreed to split the check, but when the check came,
> she refused to pay anything.

To whom is "she" referring, Nevea of Phoenicia? This needs to be cleared up.

Example₂:

> Each person thinks it is their right to choose freely their own spouse.

Here there is a plural pronoun, "their," when the subject, "each person," is singular. More and more this is becoming acceptable today, though it shouldn't: Plural pronouns refer to plural nouns.

Example₃:

> Every person should do his duty to society.

This is often seen to be sexist today. Often people say, "Every person should do his or her duty to society." This is inelegant and wordy, but there are not many happy alternatives. Perhaps the best one is to choose plural nouns and pronouns: "All people should do their duty to society."

Example₄:

> S/he can do without friends.

Again, this is quite inelegant. Choose "he" or "she," or perhaps better still, stick with the plural pronoun "they" in all instances and avoid these sticky difficulties.

C) Who and Whom

Some examples will suffice here. As a rule, the pronouns "who" and "whom" should follow the noun that they are modifying.

Amy, *who* was a constant participant in rugby matches, played viciously and aimlessly.

Amy, *whom* the crowd loved to boo, finally quit the team.

Alexander fell in love with Roxanne, *who* had earlier snubbed his advances.

Alexander fell in love with Roxanne, *whom* he had earlier detested.

"Renquist gave to ring to *whomever*" (since "whomever" follows a preposition) instead of "Renquist gave the ring to whoever."

"Renquist gave the ring to *whoever* wanted it" (since "whoever," though following a preposition, is the subject of the phrase following it).

There you'll find Aristander, *whom* you'll see you can trust to interpret your dream.

D) Which and That

Choose "that" for restrictive clauses and "which" for non-restrictive clauses. A restrictive clause functions to define a term further. A non-restrictive clause gives additional, non-definitional information about a term.

Restrictive Clause:

The puck, which is an exact replica of the one used during the Stanley-Cup finals, was on sale for ten dollars.

Non-Restrictive Clause:

The puck that you wanted to buy cost me ten dollars.

E) Some Other Rules to Avoid Mistakes

Always use sentences in formal writing. E.g., "A common enough belief shared by millions." This is not a sentence, but a modifying clause. Sentences must have minimally both a subject and a verb.
Never split an infinitive. "Flanders loves *to read* quickly" instead of "Flanders loves *to* quickly *read*."

Module Sixteen

A semicolon (;) separates two complete sentences that are intimately linked. A colon (:) does not. "Marcus gave the speech that won the day; Quintus bowed out willingly." "Marcus gave three speeches: one on friendship, one on love, and one on death."

Commas and periods. They are often, but not always, placed inside of the last of two quotation marks. "Angela is not angry," Pomona said, "she's merely being intellectual."

"The man with the red suit is me" should read "The man with the red suit is I." The verb "to be" always takes the nominative case. "It is I" and not "It is me."

When a grouping of words is used together as an adjective, hyphenate this grouping. "Nikon is a dyed-in-the-wool anarchist at heart."

In general, avoid beginning a sentence with a conjunction such as "yet," "but," or "and." Conjunctions such as "moreover" and "furthermore" are not problematic.

Never end a sentence with a preposition. E.g., "Evolution is the topic about which I wanted to talk" in preference to "Evolution is the topic I wanted to talk about." In common speaking, however, the former can seem somewhat stuffy.

Never preface a direct quote with the word "that." This word should be used when you paraphrase what someone has said, not when you quote from that person. E.g., "Shelly says that 'Justice is the most important virtue'" should read either as "Shelly says, 'Justice is the most important virtue'" or as "Shelly says that justice is the most important virtue.'"

2) OTHER COMMON MISTAKES

A) Misusing Words

Stay away from "and/or." This is tedious and affects the flow of text. "Khaled or Neh, perhaps both, went to buy milk," in preference to "Khaled and/or Neh went to buy the milk."

"Like" functions before nouns and pronouns ("Petronia eats meats like pork, chicken, and beef"), while "as" is used before phrases and clauses ("Petronia ate all her food, as is proper for a little girl").

"Can" refers to ability or potentiality; "may" relates to permission. "Tania can possibly . . . " is redundant. Simply write "Tania can . . . "

"Can not" is one word: "cannot."

Avoid all colloquialisms (street words). "Azriel's attractive" instead of "Azriel's a phat dude."

"Irregardless" is not a word. Use "regardless" or "irrespective."

"It's," used possessively, is "its." As a rule remember that "it's" has only one meaning: "it is."

Choose "different from" instead of "different than."

"Criterion" is the singular of this noun; "criteria" is its plural. The same goes for "phenomenon" and "phenomena."

Roads are "tortuous" (i.e., twisty); prison cells and classes on critical reasoning are "torturous."

"Beersham is the most unique athlete." "Unique" does not admit of degrees. Instead, "Beersham is a unique athlete."

Avoid "lots of" and use "much."

Choose "between" when referring to two things; otherwise use "among."

Avoid, at all costs, the use of "etc." in formal essay-writing. Either give a complete listing of items or narrow your list by saying something like "Philosophers—such as Plato, Aristotle, and Epicurus—valued justice highly."

"Comprise" does not mean "compose." Use it to mean "is composed of." E.g.: "Animals comprise a circulatory system and a respiratory system."

"If you like coffee, *than* you'll like this blend." Conditionals are designated by "if . . . , then . . . " and not "if . . . , than." "Than" is used for comparisons. "Five is greater *than* four."

"Allude" does not mean "elude."

Avoid the use of qualifiers, such as "rather," "very," "little," "basically," and "somewhat." E.g., "That was a pretty good effort." The word "pretty" does more to confuse than clarify the meaning.

"Disinterested" does not mean "uninterested." The latter means "having no interest," while the former means "having no passion," which is consistent with having interest.

"Further" relates to time or quantity; "farther" relates to distance.

"Literal" and "literally" are sometimes used wrongly for exaggeration. E.g., "Roxanne literally made him cry" does not add anything to "Roxanne made him cry."

Stay away in most cases from the word "interesting." E.g., "Jung's theory of dreams is interesting." This follows from the fact you are writing about it. Moreover, this begs the question: In what ways? State what is interesting about it at first.

Never use the phrase "I partially agree" and similar phrases. State just what it is you agree with and what it is you disagree with.

"Possess" is not spelled "posses." Computer programs today all have spell check options. Use them. Spelling mistakes show a teacher that you were in a rush or were too lazy to check over your paper.

Stay away from words like "declares," "promulgates," and "proclaims" when quoting another author. Use instead "says" or "states."

Never use exclamation points (!) in formal philosophical writing.

When used possessively, "one's" is apostrophized.

Write out all abbreviations, with the following exceptions: "ca." for *circa*, "e.g." (*exampli gratia*) for "for example," "et al." for *et alii* (and others), "ibid." for *ibidem* (in the same place), "vol." or "vols." for "volume" and its plural.

B) Mistakes Peculiar to Philosophy Essays

Stay away from the word "logical." To say of something that it is logical is to say that there is no contradiction involved in its use, which is a very minimal statement. Choose instead something like "reasonable" or "sensible."

In general, stay away from the word "validity," when writing. It has a technical sense in deductive reasoning and is out of place in other uses—especially in papers on philosophy. Validity is used to assess deductive arguments, not statements. It is wrong to say "The statement has no validity"; say instead, "The statement is false."

There is no need to modify the verb "to contradict." For instance, it is superfluous to say "This completely contradicts that." Contradictions do not admit of degrees.

Avoid the words "prove" and "demonstrate" for non-deductive arguments. These make for very strong claims. Instead of, "In this paper, I prove . . . " choose "In this paper, I argue . . . " Instead of, "Since Corbin hasn't shown up the last three times, this proves that he won't show up this time" choose "Since Corbin hasn't shown up the last three times, it is probable he won't show up this time."

"Enormity" has to do with morally condemnable actions. When referring to something's awesome size, choose "enormousness." The former is essentially a philosophical term; the latter is not.

"Infer" does not mean "imply." Use "imply" for sentences or statements (e.g., "'All philosophers are lovers of wisdom' implies that Aristotle is a lover of wisdom"). Use "infer" for mental activity (e.g., "Holmes inferred from the size of the hat that the owner was highly intellectual").

The word "philosophy," properly used, does not have a plural sense. It refers to the discipline in which philosophers are engaged. It makes no more sense to say "their philosophies . . . " than it does to say "their biologies . . . " or "their psychologies . . . " So, instead of "the philosophies of the two men . . . " choose something like "the ideas of the two men . . . " or "the accounts of the two men . . . "

"Justice" contrasts with "injustice"; "just" with "unjust."

Review what is said about modal words, words indicative of possibility and necessity, in module nine at this point.

Section Six

WRITING PHILOSOPHICAL ESSAYS

Module Seventeen

Evaluative Essays

1) OBJECT OF AN EVALUATIVE ESSAY

The object of an evaluative essay is to develop a thesis that critically addresses, in a short essay, one work (or some part of it, say, one argument) of a particular philosopher. You may be in complete agreement, partial agreement, or complete disagreement with what this author has to say. The point is to argue for your thesis by using evidence and reasons. Also, try not to do too much with your thesis—especially for short papers. Being overly ambitious is usually a recipe for disaster.

2) STEPS FOR WRITING AN EVALUATIVE ESSAY

A) Write Out Your Thesis.

Your thesis tells readers what you'll be arguing for. Use this as a guide for the entire essay. You may find that, while writing, you wish to narrow it down—that is, make it more concise and specific. However, once you've settled on a thesis that is sufficient for the task you've undertaken, never stray from it.

B) Incorporate Your Thesis in a Brief Introductory Paragraph.

For a very short essay (e.g., one-to-two pages in length), make this introduction very brief. Get to the point quickly. Often two sentences suffice: the first to set up the thesis, the other to present the thesis.

Example:

> At *Apology* 25c–26b, Socrates gives the second of three main arguments
> against his accuser Meletus. In this paper, I maintain that this argument in
> itself is enough to show that Meletus is unfit to charge and prosecute
> Socrates of corrupting the young.

For longer essays, a lengthier introduction is better. This enables you to
set up the problem you wish to discuss with utmost clarity.

Example:

> *Apology* is a work by Plato that chronicles the life of Socrates through his
> trial for his life. Being accused of corrupting the young, Socrates stands
> in defense before two sets of accusers: those older and those younger.
> Plato gives an especially vivid account of Socrates' cross-examination of
> the main representative of the younger accusers—a man named Meletus,
> who will, as it turns out, be chiefly responsible for the death of Socrates.
>   While examining Meletus, Socrates himself puts forth three arguments
> that are designed cleverly to show that Meletus is ignorant of just those
> matters about which he charges Socrates and, thus, he is not fit to prose-
> cute Socrates. At *Apology* 25c–26b, Plato gives the second of these
> three—an especially cunning argument aimed to expose Meletus' igno-
> rance. In this paper, I maintain that this argument in itself is enough to
> show that Socrates should not have been on trial for the crimes of which
> he was accused.

C) Summarize Any Arguments You Are Addressing.

Quote directly only if there is something unique about an author's wording that paraphrasing cannot capture. For example, when you wish to
show that an author commits the fallacy of ambiguity, you should quote
her so that you can show your readers precisely how she commits this
fallacy. When summarizing an argument, use the *principle of charity*:

Always restate an argument that is being evaluated in its strongest pos-
sible formulation.

This greatly reduces any possibility of misrepresenting that position. In-
tentional misrepresentation for the sake of easy refutation is called
"building up a straw man" (see module twelve).

D) Critically Examine the Argument.

What are the points of agreement, if any? Just what do you find objectionable? Examine the best arguments of the thesis you are addressing. In doing so, of course, you will be putting forth arguments of your own. Present all arguments with an eye to maximum clarity. This, of course, also means that simplicity of expression is of utmost importance. Clarity and simplicity enable you to communicate convincingly with the greatest possible audience.

E) Reference All Material, Whether Paraphrasing or Quoting.

Examples:

1) In one study of two groups of athletes—those who professed to use amply psychological tactics in athletic performance and those who claimed that they never use such tactics—no statistically significant differences were found in overall performance of both groups (Bunderkrufts 2001, 69).

2) Freud believes that god the father is a free creation of our wish impulses and has no basis in reality (1966, 67).

The first example refers to a particular study. The author's name, not mentioned in the text, is given in parentheses, along with the year and the page of the published work in which it is to be found. In the second example, since Freud is mentioned in the text, his name need not be placed prior to the year of his work.

F) Summarize Your Argument.

Walk readers through a brief summary of your entire argument at paper's end. This should be limited to one short paragraph for short papers. As a general (though not inviolable) rule, keep the length of your summary consistent with the length of your introduction.

Example (back to Plato's *Apology*, short-essay example):

In this essay, I have argued that the second argument that Socrates puts forth against Meletus in his defense is the strongest of the three. I hope to have shown that this argument should have been sufficient to exonerate Socrates from the charge of corrupting the young.

G) Include a Title.

This must be informative and it can be clever. Never try to be cute at the expense of being informative.

Example (again from Plato's *Apology*):

Was Socrates' Death Sentence Just?

H) Include a Bibliography.

There are several ways to do this. I illustrate just one. Consult your instructor for her preference. Whichever way you choose, just be sure to include all the necessary information. I make up two below.

Article:

Babcock, T. Frantley. (2000). "Tonsured Tops and Type B Personality." *Journal in Support of Ill-Funded Psychological Research,* I. New York: Algpoitch & Daughters Publishers, Inc., 35–50.

Book:

Witherwirk, Krensella. (2000). *The Complete Party Guide for Agoraphobics.* Kalamazoo, MI: Serenity Press of America.

Note: Always write up a publishing company *precisely* as it appears in a publication. If a company appears as "Smyntner & Smythe, Publishers Inc.," then rewrite is just as it is—ampersand (&) and all. In addition, for publishers in American cities that are not commonly known, always include the state (i.e., its two-letter abbreviation) after the city. For instance, in the first example, "New York" is not followed by "NY," while in the second, "Kalamazoo" is followed by "MI," since it is likely that many if not most people do not know where Kalamazoo is.

Appendix B gives a student's sample outline and essay for a short evaluative essay on Epicurus' views on justice and friendship.

Module Eighteen

Critical Essays

1) OBJECT OF A CRITICAL ESSAY

A critical essay is a larger project than an evaluative essay. In the latter, you do no more than evaluate the philosophical position of a single author on a particular issue. For a critical essay, you must draw from more than one source of the existing philosophical literature on some issue (usually, the literature introduced in the classroom will be sufficient) and, most importantly, develop *your own thesis*. In other words, in a critical essay, you go beyond mere criticism of others' views and put forth your own view. In general, about half of your paper should relate to what *you* think about an issue. Note that much of what is covered in module seventeen applies here as well.

2) STEPS FOR WRITING A CRITICAL ESSAY

A) Address What Others Have to Say on Your Topic.

When drawing from other sources, take from the best or most recent views and offer a critical analysis of this material, insofar as it has impacted the development of your thought. For larger essays, you may do this briefly prior to your thesis and more fully in the body of the text later.

B) Write Out Your Thesis in the Introductory Paragraph.

Remember, you are trying to draw in readers with this introduction. Make it interesting. Be clear also how your view differs from that of

other philosophers you will be criticizing. I give two examples below
for illustration.

Example$_1$:

> The topic "happiness" has traditionally been and continues to be the focal
> point of and most seductive issue in philosophical discussions in ethics.
> While many, such as Aristotle and Mill, take it to be the end of all human
> activity, almost all (if not all) philosophers acknowledge that it is a valu-
> able, if not essential, component of a good life.
>
> Happiness proves puzzling, however. Though we all desire it, few of us
> seem to be able to secure it. The question becomes: Why is something that
> is so slippery so desirable?
>
> In this essay, I do not wish to solve the puzzle of happiness. I merely
> give reasons why it exists. *My paper will center on a notion of happiness
> being a nesting of three different types of integration: personal, political,
> and cosmic.*

Note: The puzzle of happiness is a sufficiently broad issue—too broad
for even a 20-page essay. Therefore, it is appropriate here to tell readers
just what cannot be done in this paper.

Example$_2$ (student's paper, "Philosophy of Sport"):

> To begin I would like to pose a few questions to you, the reader. Who lost
> the NCAA basketball championship five years ago? Who was beat out in
> the presidential election in 1992? Who was the first team eliminated in the
> 2002 Stanley Cup Playoffs? You may be wondering why anyone would
> even be interested in trying to answer any of these questions. I am fairly
> certain that the majority of readers (at least those who follow sports and
> observe politics) would be able to answer any of these questions if they
> were slightly modified. For instance, who was the winner of the NCAA
> basketball championship five years ago, or who won our presidential elec-
> tion in 1992? By simply changing the subject from the loser to the win-
> ner, we suddenly have a better recollection and associate a greater impor-
> tance to the answer.

In the next paragraph, this student comments on how we lionize winners and forget all others who don't win—even those people and teams
who were very close to wining it all. This speaks to his thesis concerning an unhealthy obsession with winning in American society.

This is a very clever introduction to an intriguing philosophical issue. It seduces you as a reader by challenging your memory and the challenge sets up the thesis. After reading this introduction, I certainly wanted to read further.

C) Flesh Out Your Adversaries' Views.

Remember, be charitable. Give their best arguments and make doubly sure that there is no misrepresentation of their views. Again, if there is something about an author's own presentation of an argument that you want to address (e.g., ambiguous use of a word or vagueness), you may want to present this argument in the author's own words.

D) Expose the Weaknesses of These Views.

Why is it that these views cannot be maintained philosophically?

Example:

> Freud maintains that happiness is the immediate satisfaction of dammed up erotic impulses. This view, however, is much too narrow. *First*, it fails to capture anything of current linguistic usage. *Moreover*, it conflates the pleasure that is attendant upon sexual release with happiness. This reduces happiness to a type of erotic hedonism that leaves no room for the happiness that attends upon intellectual or aesthetic pursuits. For these reasons, Freud's view cannot be maintained.

E) Present Your Own View and Give Arguments on Behalf of It.

Knocking down contrary views is not enough to defend a thesis. You need to motivate your own view in a positive fashion—i.e., to show why your view is philosophically superior to other views. How does it solve problems or address issues that other views cannot?

F) Point Out Any Weaknesses or Deficiencies of Your Own View.

State conceivable objections to your view and show how these can be remedied. If some objections cannot be remedied fully, show how your view is still preferable to the other theses you have criticized.

Practice Exercise: Take a contentious statement that you believe to be true (e.g., "God exists," "The state governs best which governs least," or "The taking of human life through abortion is never morally acceptable") and do your best to argue *against* it ("God *doesn't* exist," "*It's false that* the state governs best which governs least," or "The taking of human life through abortion is *sometimes* morally acceptable"). Give as many arguments as you can. Examine thoroughly *all* the conceptual space in this exercise.

G) Summarize Your Argument.

Do this at the very end of the paper. Again, the summary should roughly be of the same length as the introduction. One paragraph is usually sufficient for a short essay.

Appendix C gives a student's sample outline and essay for a short critical essay on the obsession with winning in American sport.

Module Nineteen

Revising and Rewriting Essays

This brief, final module addresses what is very often overlooked in courses on philosophy: revising and rewriting essays. As with so many other disciplines, success in writing a good philosophical essay is a matter of toil and a little sweat. Even for professional philosophers, getting published, especially in the best journals, is difficult. Persistence is the key. Success usually comes through rewriting papers by addressing the comments of colleagues or reviewers. This means that a highly polished paper generally undergoes many revisions. It is the same with writing philosophical essays for class. Don't expect to write a perfect paper in one draft; this won't happen, even for the best students. Ask colleagues to read and give a critical response to your paper. Do the same for their paper. You may be frustrated at first to find that you seem to be making so many mistakes and that there is so much to learn about writing a solid philosophical essay. Yet keep plugging away, and you'll see improvement with each effort. Be patient. By term's end, you'll be surprised to see just how much you have learned about writing a tight philosophical essay.

In what follows, I offer some suggestions on revising and rewriting your philosophical essay that have proven effective in my own classes over the years. You might devise your own plan or consult with your instructor about ideas he might have.

1) REVISION ONE

Plan out your essay so that you'll finish it a few days in advance of its deadline. Let the paper sit for a day or two, and move on to other projects.

After a couple of days, go back to your paper with a renewed and reinvigorated effort. Inspect the outline for tightness of thesis and, throughout, coherence of thought. Look for tightness and cogency in your arguments on behalf of your thesis. Go through the spell-check menu. Look for problems with grammar. Inspect the bibliography for completeness. Look over your title. Have a friend or colleague do the same. Write down all the problems with your essay on a separate sheet of paper. You or your reader can use a comment sheet like the one given in Appendix D. Rewrite the paper to address the problems.

2) REVISION TWO

This revision should be done in the classroom. Bring in two drafts of your paper. Under the direction of your teacher, break into circular groups of, say, three. In clockwise fashion, hand a copy of your paper for critical commentary to the person to your left, while your group members follow likewise (i.e., you receive the paper of the person to your right). Use a photocopy of the comment sheet given in Appendix D for your comments on colleagues' papers. When this has been completed, hand the other copy of your paper to the person to your right to get a second set of comments on your paper (while the two others do the same).

When both sets of comments have been completed, collect these, read them thoroughly (not all will be substantive), and set up a written plan for revising your essay in agreement with these comments. Appendix E is a sample sheet for setting up such a plan. Revise your paper accordingly.

Appendix A

Exercises for Diagramming

Here are some practice exercises to sharpen your evaluative skills through diagramming. Use the tips of module seven and diagram each of the following examples in the space directly beneath it.

"It is not too much to say that an educational philosophy which professes to be based on the idea of freedom may become as dogmatic as ever was the traditional education which is reacted against. For any theory and set of practices is dogmatic which is not based upon critical examination of its own underlying principles." (John Dewey, *Experience and Education*)

"It is desirable, in short, that in things which do not primarily concern others, individuality should assert itself. Where not the person's own character but the traditions or customs of other people are the rule of conduct, there is wanting one of the principle ingredients of human happiness and the chief ingredient of individual and social progress." (John Stuart Mill, *On Liberty*)

"It seems to me that it is an excellent thing for a physician to practice prognosis. For, if he has foreknowledge and declares beforehand at his patients' beside both the present, the past, and the future, filling in the details they have omitted, it will be believed that he has a better understanding of their cases so that they will have the confidence to entrust themselves to him as their doctor. Furthermore, he would carry out treatment most effectively from foreknowledge derived from the present symptoms of what will be the future course of the disease." (Hippocratic author of *Prognostics*)

"A little reflection will show that civil disobedience is a necessary part of non-cooperation. You assist an administration most effectively by obeying its orders and decrees. An evil administration never deserves such allegiance. Allegiance to it means partaking of evil. A good man will resist an evil system or administration with his whole soul." (Mohandas Gandhi)

"If there is some deceiver or other who is supremely powerful and supremely sly and who is always deliberately deceiving me, then I still know that I exist. For let him do his best at deception, he will never bring it about that I am nothing so long as I shall think that I am something. Thus, after this and all other arguments have been most carefully weighed, it must finally be established that this pronouncement 'I am, I exist' is necessarily true every time I utter it or conceive it in my mind." (René Descartes, *Meditations*)

"Though in the state of nature he has a right to property, yet the enjoyment of it is very uncertain, and constantly exposed to the invasion of others: for all being kings as much as he, every man his equal, and the greater part no strict observers of equity and justice, the enjoyment of the property he has in this state is very unsafe, very unsecure." (John Locke, *Second Treatise on Government*)

"I am persuaded that those who quite sincerely attribute their sorrows to their views about the universe are putting the cart before the horse: the truth is that they are unhappy for some reason of which they are unaware, and this unhappiness leads them to dwell upon the less agreeable characteristics of the world in which they live." (Bertrand Russell, *Conquest of Happiness*)

"To fear death, gentlemen, is no other than to think oneself wise when one is not, to think one knows what one does not know. No one knows whether death may not be the greatest of all blessings for a man, yet men fear it as if they knew that it is the greatest of evils. And surely it is the most blameworthy ignorance to believe that one knows what one does not know." (Plato, *Apology*)

"So powerful a prohibition (i.e., taboo versus incest or killing) can only be directed against an equally powerful impulse. What no human soul desires stands in no need of prohibition; it is excluded automatically. The very emphasis laid on the commandment 'Thou shalt not kill' makes it certain that we spring from an endless series of generations of murderers, who had the lust for killing in their blood, as, perhaps, we ourselves have today." (Sigmund Freud, "Thoughts for the Times on War and Death")

"The peace that it [a just war] establishes must be a clear improvement over what exists. Although there are visions of peace and democracy in Iraq, it is quite possible that the aftermath of a military invasion will destabilize the region and prompt terrorists to further jeopardize our security at home. Also, by defying overwhelming world opposition, the United States will undermine the United Nations as a viable institution for world peace." (Jimmy Carter, "Just War—or a Just War?" *The New York Times*, March 9, 2003)

Appendix B

Evaluative Essay and Outline

ASSIGNED QUESTION

What is justice for Epicurus? What is friendship? Critically assess the relationship between these two virtues in Epicurean society.

OUTLINE

I) Thesis: In the following essay, I explain what justice and friendship are for Epicurus, and point out a problem that exists with the virtue of friendship and how it goes against the very basis of his hedonism.

II) Epicurus on Justice
   a) Egoistic hedonism, justice, and pleasure
   b) Justice is an agreement
   c) Why people are just
   d) How justice is the same for everyone
   e) How justice differs between societies

III) Epicurus on Friendship
   a) Friendship is held in high regard
   b) Friendship goes against egoistic hedonism
   c) Friendship is chosen for its own sake
   d) Epicurus advocates altruism toward friends

IV) Summary

V) Bibliography

ESSAY: EPICURUS, JUSTICE, AND FRIENDSHIP
BY MICHELE S. HERDOIZA

In the following essay, I explain what justice and friendship are for Epicurus. I then point out a problem that exists with the virtue of friendship and how it goes against the very basis of Epicureanism because it is choice-worthy due to its altruistic nature instead of its immediate pleasure.

Epicurus is an egoistic hedonist who advocates that justice is done entirely for the sake of one's own pleasure. Justice is an agreement between people of a society "neither to harm or be harmed" (*PD* 31). Epicurus believes that the only reason members of society are not unjust is due to their fear of being caught, the fear alone of being caught is enough to cause a person great anxiety, which he says is "The fundamental obstacle of happiness" (vii). Yet which actions and principles are considered just vary according to each particular society. Each society devises its own laws that are useful, and, in turn, only the laws that are useful for that society are just. "And if someone passes a law and it does not turn out to be in accord with what is useful in mutual associations, this no longer possesses the nature of justice" (*PD* 37). Therefore, the laws that are useful for one society are different from the laws of other societies, and can also differ with the passing of time. To put it another way, all cultures use rules, but the rules that are just differ and change with place and time.

The virtue of friendship is held in high regard by Epicurus and is greatly praised and valued. "Of the things which wisdom provides for the blessedness of one's whole life, by far the greatest is the possession of friendship" (*PD* 27). Yet the virtue of friendship is unclear because it seems to go against the egoistic hedonism that Epicurus advocates. Here he clearly states that friendship is not worth choosing for pleasure, "Every friendship is worth choosing for its own sake, thought it takes its origin from the benefits [it confers on us]" (*SV* 23). It seems as though Epicurus advocates altruism toward friends. Through friendships individuals are able to trust each other, to give and receive help, and to support emotionally each other by promoting confidence and encouragement. Friendships also help individuals fight their insecurities and provide great emotional strength. True friends treat each other with respect, and would do no differently for each other than they would do for themselves. According to Epicurus, a wise man "will sometimes die for a friend" (*Lives* 121b).

Epicureanism preaches that justice and morality ultimately rest on one's own self-interests, on one's devotion to pleasure and self-gratification. In turn, a person will choose to do an action because it leads directly to one's own immediate pleasure, not for the sake of the actions itself. Because of this, the virtue of friendship in Epicurean thought becomes a confusing issue due to its altruistic nature. Although Epicurus does state that friendship is choice-worthy due to the immediate pleasure one derives from it, he also says that friendship is worth choosing for its own sake, not for pleasure. He does this by expounding upon the reasons why individuals choose friendship, therefore leading one to believe that the virtue of friendship goes against his teachings that all actions are done for the sake of pleasure.

WORK CITED

Epicurus. (1994). *The Epicurus Reader: Selected Writings and Testimonia.* Brad Inwood and L. P. Gerson (trans. and eds.). Indianapolis: Hackett Publishing Company, Inc.

Appendix C

Critical Essay and Outline

ASSIGNED QUESTION

There was no assigned question. This student chose to write on the American obsession with winning in competitive sport.

OUTLINE

I) Thesis: Overemphasizing the outcome of performance and downplaying the performance itself is a corruption of modern sport.

II) Two Notions of "Success"
   a) "Success" as Winning
   b) "Success" as Effort

III) Neo-Marxist View
   a) Play becomes Work
   b) Success = External Rewards
   c) Downplaying Internal Rewards

IV) Internal-Rewards View
   a) Set Reachable Goals for Self, Team
   b) Seek Inner Satisfaction
   c) Problem of Youth Sports

ESSAY: AMERICA'S OBSESSION WITH WINNING
BY SAMANTHA PFALLER

"Winning is not everything; it's the only thing." These words of Vince Lombardi, legendary coach of the Green Bay Packers, echo the importance American society places on winning. America's obsession with winning stems from equating success with winning. For example, in the 2002 Winter Olympics, the judges admitted to fixing the pairs-skating scores, which resulted in the Canadian skaters not winning the gold. When a win-loss record is the only gauge for athletic success, attitudes toward athletic competition may easily shift from "It is not whether you win or lose; it is how you play the game" to "It's not how you play the game; just that you win!" (Hudley 2002, 206). Overemphasizing the outcome of performance and downplaying the performance itself is a corruption of modern sport.

The problem is that winning is overemphasized, and, as a result, individual achievement and athletic excellence do not receive proper appreciation and acknowledgement. Hundley writes, "Great performances, efforts, and special feelings of personal and team achievements are often not acknowledged after a defeat" (2002, 206). As a society, we seem to have a preconceived notion that if you are number one, only then have you won and only then are you successful.

There are at least two possible perspectives of what winning is: one based on outcome and one based on effort. Unfortunately, the societal perception of winning weighs heavily and almost entirely on the perspective of winning determined exclusively on the basis of the final score. Accordingly, losing is equated with failing to dominate other athletes—failing to finish first. Instead, as I'll try to show in what follows, the individual and team should be perceived as winners when they perform and compete to the best of their ability, regardless of the final outcome.

The desire to win is a necessary part of competitive sport, but why not also compete for the sake of competitive spirit and enjoyment, as opposed to the tangible extrinsic payoff? In modern sport, there seems to be little competition for the sheer enjoyment of competition—that is, for sheer play; most everything in sport, as in society at large, is done for the sake of external reward as a motive. Athletes compete to obtain money, fitness, fame, and records. Following the neo-Marxist view of sport, "Play is perceived as a means of fulfilling some other need; hence play is reduced to another form of work" (Hundley 2002, 213). Sport mirrors the society it serves and adopts its attitudes, norms, and values. In capitalistic societies, sport becomes another form of production and achievement—essentially another form of work.

When sport is seen as a form of production or work, the problem is that ends overwhelm means. The extrinsic rewards of athletic competition overshadow the internal rewards. We see this especially in the overemphasis on statistical data in sports magazines and journals, which act to further distance us from a perception of winning as physical excellence. This is the problem with competitive sport in America.

As a society, we need to redefine success. Putting winning and losing into a more sober perspective, an athlete should be considered successful in terms of what goals the individual sets. The realization that "winning is not the be all and the end all of athletic excellence may help to foster the cooperation that is part of healthy competition and prevent it from degenerating into alienation" (Dixon 2002, 232). The key is to set goals that aren't out of sight and unattainable. These goals will act to inspire the individual to strive toward human physical excellence through sportsmanship and fair play. Achieving one's goals makes an athlete victorious and successful, and these goals need not include being number one.

By redefining success, athletes will be content with their individual achievements and the collective team achievements, when they strive for physical excellence and compete with sportsmanship, regardless of the outcome of a game or a season. Victory would be a matter of the inner satisfaction of knowing that you have done your best or given all that you could have given. Furthermore, by redefining success, athletic dishonesty in the form of cheating, trash-talking, and other distasteful forms of gamesmanship would largely disappear from sports, as winning wouldn't be sought by any means whatsoever.

Unfortunately, today, from an early age, athletes quickly learn to associate success with winning. They are taught that losing is something bad and that losers are nobodies. Moreover, individuals are taught that hard work is the root of all success, and that failure to come out on top is a sign of a lack of work (Hundley 2002, 209–11). The problem with a heightened regard for winning is that individual pride and sense of achievement are completely eliminated if a competitor falls short of attaining superiority over other athletes. Only winners are entitled to feel good about themselves, but the very nature of competitive sport prevents the great majority from winning. Moreover, the best athletes don't always win, due to cheating, refereeing errors, or even bad luck.

In order to redefine success in sport, we need to reform athletes' attitudes toward it. To do this, their coaches (and parents) need to change how they think about success, since the attitudes and values of these are instilled in their players. For instance, if a coach believes that coming in first is the only worthwhile achievement, then athletes will be hard pressed to learn that sport can teach them anything else. Under such a coach, most athletes will quickly develop feelings of underachievement and inadequacy. Hence, it is extremely important that coaches of younger athletes, from little league to high-school sports, have some knowledge of child psychology. Yet, since there is also great risk of physical damage to young athletes, they need knowledge of physiology of exercise and motor development too. Competitive sport should be both challenging and fun, and coaches should create an athletic environment that emphasizes participation more than achievement. Children especially should be able to experience the joy of participation for its own sake—play for the sake of play.

Today's American athletes are obsessed with winning. What should be play has become a form of work. This is especially tragic in the case of children's sports. We as a society need to sit back and rethink the notion of success in competitive sport in order to create a healthier and saner view of the athletic experience. After all, ends do not entirely justify the means: How you play the game counts for quite a bit too.

WORKS CITED

Hundley, Joan. (2002). "The Overemphasis on Winning: A Philosophical Look." *Philosophy of Sport: Critical Readings, Crucial Issues.* Upper Saddle River, NJ: Prentice Hall.

Dixon, Nicholas. (2002). "On Winning and Athletic Superiority." *Philosophy of Sport: Critical Readings, Crucial Issues.* Upper Saddle River, NJ: Prentice Hall.

Appendix D

Teacher/Student Comment Sheet

Read the essay you receive twice. First, read it without an eye for criticism. Try to get a general grasp of the thesis, the main line of argument, and the overall coherence of the essay. Read it then a second time, and prepare a critical commentary guided by the categories below. Use the back of this paper, if needed.

1) Comments on the thesis:

2) Comments on arguments on behalf of thesis:

3) Comments on use of text(s):

4) Comments on structure and coherence of paper:

5) Comments on grammar, spelling, etc.:

Appendix E

Plan-for-Revision Sheet

Read carefully all of the comments given by students or the teacher (or both). Respond to comments in each category below. Even if comments for a particular category are generally favorable, you still ought to have something to say concerning improvement, however slight, about that category.

1) Reconsideration of my thesis:

2) Reconsideration of arguments on behalf of my thesis:

3) Reconsideration of my use of text(s):

4) Reconsideration of the structure and coherence of my paper:

5) Reconsideration of grammar, spelling, etc.:

Bibliography

Abelard, Peter. *The Story of My Misfortune*. Trans. Henry Adam Bellows. New York: Macmillan, 1972.

Addelson, Kathryn Pyne. "Equality and Competition: Can Sports Make a Women of a Girl?" In *Women, Philosophy, and Sport: A Collection of New Essays*, 133–61. Metuchen, NJ: Scarecrow Press, 1983.

Aristotle. *Nicomachean Ethics*. 2d ed. Trans. Terrence Irwin. Indianapolis: Hackett, 1999.

——. *On the Heavens*. Trans. W. K. C. Guthrie. Cambridge: Harvard University Press, 1986.

——. *Politics*. Trans. C. D. C. Reeve. Indianapolis: Hackett, 1998.

Brzezinski, Zbigniew. *The Grand Failure: The Birth and Death of Communism in the Twentieth Century*. New York: Scribner, 1989.

Camus, Albert. *The Fall*. New York: Knopf, 1957.

Carter, Jimmy. "Just War—or a Just War?" *New York Times*, March 9, 2003.

Damer, T. Edward. *Attacking Faulty Reasoning*. 4th ed. Belmont, CA: Wadsworth, 2001.

Darwin, Charles. *Origin of Species*. New York: New York University Press, 1988.

Descartes, René. *Meditations on First Philosophy*. 3d ed. Trans. Donald A. Cress. Indianapolis: Hackett, 1993).

Dewey, John. *Experience and Education*. New York: Simon & Shuster, 1997.

Diogenes. *Lives*. Vol. 2. Trans. R. D. Hicks. Cambridge: Harvard University Press, 1991.

Edwards, Anne Michael. *Writing to Learn: An Introduction to Writing Philosophical Essays*. Boston: McGraw-Hill Higher Education, 2000.

Epicurus. *Principle Doctrines* in *The Epicurus Reader*. Eds. Brad Inwood and L. P. Gerson. Indianapolis: Hackett, 1994.

Feinberg, Joel. *Doing Philosophy: A Guide to the Writing of Philosophy Papers*. 2d ed. Belmont, CA: Wadsworth, 2002.

Fisher, Alec. *The Logic of Real Arguments*. Cambridge University Press, 1998.

Freud, Sigmund. "Reflections upon War and Death." In *Character and Culture*. Ed. Philip Rieff. New York: Macmillan, 1963.

Gandhi, Mohatma. *Selected Political Writings*. Ed. Dennis Dalton. Indianapolis: Hackett, 1996.

Hippocrates. *On Prognosis*. Trans. W. H. S. Jones. *Hippocrates*. Vol. 2. Loeb Classical Library. Cambridge, MA: Harvard University Press, 1923.

Homer. *Iliad*. Trans. Richard Lattimore. Chicago: University of Chicago Press, 1961.

James, William. *Pragmatism—A New Name for Some Old Ways of Thinking*. New York: Longmans, Green and Co., 1943.

Jefferson, Thomas. "The Letters of Thomas Jefferson: 1743–1826: To Thomas Law Poplar Forest, June 1814." Available at odur.let.rug.nl/~usa/P/tj3/writings/brf/jefl230.htm (accessed October 3, 2003).

Jung, C. G. "On the Significance of Number Dreams." In *Dreams*. Ed. Gerhard Adler. Princeton, NJ: Princeton University Press, 1974.

Kant, Immanuel. *Grounding for the Metaphysics of Morals*. Trans. James W. Ellington. Indianapolis: Hackett, 1993.

Locke, John *Second Treatise of Government*. Ed. Thomas P. Peardon. New York: Macmillan.

Luke, Carmen, and Jennifer Gore. *Feminisms and Critical Pedagogy*. New York: Routledge, 1992.

Malcolm, Norman. *Dreaming*. London: Routledge & Paul, 1964.

Mill, John Stuart. *On Liberty*. New York: Penguin, 1985.

Nussbaum, Martha. *The Therapy of Desire: Theory and Practice in Hellenistic Ethics*. Princeton, NJ: Princeton University Press, 1994.

Plato. *Apology*. In *Five Dialogues*. Trans. G. M. A. Grube. Indianapolis: Hackett, 1981.

———. *Laches*. In *Laches and Charmides*. Trans. Rosamond Kent Sprague. Indianapolis: Hackett, 1992.

Rosenberg, Jay F. *The Practice of Philosophy*. 3d ed. Upper Saddle River, NJ: Prentice-Hall, 1996.

Russell, Bertrand. *Conquest of Happiness*. New York: Liveright, 1958.

Schick, Theodore, Jr., and Lewis Vaughn. *How to Think about Weird Things*. Mountain View, CA: Mayfield Publishing Company, 1995.

Sextus, Empiricus. *Selections*. Ed. Phillip Hallie. Indianapolis: Hackett, 1985.

Skinner, B. F. *Science and Human Behavior*. New York: Free Press, 1965.

Twain, Mark. *The Diary of Adam and Eve*. Kansas City: Hallmark Cards, 1975.

Weston, Anthony. *A Rulebook for Arguments*. 3d ed. Indianapolis: Hackett, 2000.

Index

About the Author

M. Andrew Holowchak is assistant professor of philosophy at Kutztown University in Pennsylvania and a contributing author to *Fundamentals of Philosophy*, 5th ed.